MW01230313

Protecting Your House
from Pests

Books by Jonnie Whittington

Bible Studies

Building Your House

Protecting Your House from Pests

Wives of the Bible

Biographical Historical Novels

Kidd and Spitfire Doll

Kidd's Daughter *Another Spitfire*

Kidd's Daughter Becomes a Woman

Protecting Your House from Pests

A woman's Book on Spiritual Warfare

Jonnie Whittington

Protecting Your House from Pests

Copyright © 2012

Jonnie Whittington

This book is also available as a Kindle ebook.

Visit www.amazon.com

Cover created by Jason Taylor

Scripture quotations are taken from the King James
Version of the Bible unless marked

All Rights Reserved

Library of Congress Cataloguing-in-Publication Data

ISBN 978-0-9856986-6-9 (Soft cover)

Protecting Your House from Pests

Printed in the United States of America

Dedicated to

Mike, my middle son

Table of Contents   Page

WHY WRITE ANOTHER BOOK ON

SPIRITUAL WARFARE?

"Hello," I said into the phone.

"Hello, Mama?" It was Mike, my middle son. I heard a familiar commotion in the background - loud noises. Men talked and cursed. Footsteps echoed in a hollow sounding building. Metal doors clanged. My heart beat faster.

"Mike, where are you?" I knew before he answered.

"In Kentucky," he said, "in jail."

I swallowed, my fear confirmed. I had heard those sounds before. The old feelings tried to surface. *No*, I told myself. *Don't get upset. This is only temporary.* Was that me thinking or was it the Holy Spirit? At any rate, I felt the peace of God strengthening me.

I answered him calmly, "What happened? I thought you preached at Bible School not long ago."

"I did," he said, "But then I did something stupid - again!"

I always tried to keep the lines of communication open, thinking if Mike felt free to talk to me about his problem, maybe he would also feel free to talk to God. He explained that he had relapsed, smoked crack cocaine again and as a result got into trouble. He tried to justify his actions yet knew that he had done wrong.

"Oh, Mike, I'm so sorry," I said. "It's been five years since you've used drugs or got into trouble."

"I know," he said. "I was doing good." I heard frustration as his voice grew louder. "I don't know why I had to go and get stupid and mess up again."

"I've been concerned about you since I hadn't heard from you in a while," I said. "Your roommate from school was worried too. He didn't know where you were. I'm glad you are all right. Have you talked to the Lord about it yet? You know He loves you and will help you if you ask Him."

"Yeah, I know, Mama." He sighed. He had heard that statement from me before. "I don't know how He can love me as many times as I've failed Him."

"Oh, but he does, Mike," I advised. "He never gives up on us and don't you give up on yourself."

"I better hang up. This is costing you," he said, then added, "Mama, can you send me some socks and a sweatshirt? It's real cold in here. I'll pay you back when I get out."

"Sure, Mike." He gave me the address. My eyes were dry, but my heart sad.

As I cradled the phone another thought popped into my mind. *Oh no, what will I do about the book?* I had written a book - *Building Your House* - and sent it to the publishers. It was going to press any day now. In the book, I told about Mike's deliverance from crack cocaine and that he was at World Harvest Bible College. Now, that was a lie. He evidently wasn't delivered and he definitely was not at Bible College. Should I call and tell Pathway Press not to publish the book?

It had taken me twenty years to gain confidence enough to write *Building Your House* and another two years after it was written to send it to a publisher. Pathway Press, the first one I submitted it to, said they would publish it. That was unusual. I knew God had ordained me to write the book and felt it would be used by Him especially as a teaching tool for jail and prison inmates. I had already taught from my notes at the Orange County Jail for women in Orlando, Florida. The women received the teaching and were blessed.

I couldn't stop the presses from rolling now. The book must be published. It was based on the Bible, not Mike's testimony. It was based on Jesus and His sermon on the mount. All of that was still true.

The Lord seemed to say to me, *don't worry. This is a minor setback, Mike will be okay. Satan doesn't want the book published.*

When Mike got in trouble, it had always seemed like the end of the world. Somehow I felt much different this time, I didn't cry, fall apart, or feel hopeless. I still had my joy and peace. Maybe I had finally learned to trust God completely.

I battled a few more days about whether or not to publish. Finally, I told my husband how I felt and asked his opinion.

"Jonnie, you need to publish the book."

I did. I've never been sorry.

A wonderful man from our faith and church witnessed and prayed with Mike in the jail. He made things right with God. Released in six months, he came back to Florida to live with us and was diagnosed as bipolar. He received help, and is in church every service. He learned to play the bass guitar - practically taught himself, plays for church and is a blessing. God is so faithful.

Don't ever give up on God, on your loved ones, or on yourself. Jesus loves you.

Pathway Press published *Building Your House* in 2002. I went to the Church of God General Assembly in Indianapolis for a book signing. When Dan Betzer spoke at the mission service, I felt compelled to give the book to God. All the money I make on it goes into a fund to place - *Building Your House* - into jails and prisons.

I go into churches to speak and offer the book. I have to sell two books to give one book to a girl in jail. It's hard work but well worth it. With the help of our church in Tavares, New Life Church of God, and my speaking, I have put about six hundred books in jails and prisons. It doesn't seem like much compared to the larger ministries, but God said don't compare yourself to others. Do what you can do. I believe God will help me send the book around the world.

When I walked into the jail and a girl met me and said, "I just finished reading your book. It was wonderful. Thank you!" or "I'm reading your book and it is changing my life. Thanks!" or "I love your book. It is helping me so much!" That made it all worthwhile. I'm glad I didn't stop the presses.

* * *

Soon after it was published, Annette Watson, who wrote the forward for *Building Your House* told me at a ladies luncheon, "Jonnie, now that your house is built, Satan will try to invade it. You need to write another book on how to keep the pests out of your house." She told me to write about Tala the termite, Rastas the roach, Anty the ant, and Rodie the rodent who would try to take over the finished house.

This book is my take on her suggestion. It is a book on spiritual warfare. There is no way that we should allow the destructive gnawing of Tala the termite to undermine our structure. Nor should we allow Ratley the rat or any of the other pests to destroy our peace and joy and steal our stuff.

Let's learn to keep our spiritual house . . . pest free!

PREPARATIONS

My friend, Tricia Jumpp, clutched the steering wheel of her car as she maneuvered through heavy city traffic. We were on our way home from a ladies meeting. She said, "Jonnie, I believe you and I could have a wonderful women's seminar. Have you ever thought about it?"

"Yes, I have. It's strange that you said that because Janie told me at church last Sunday that God is about to use me in a new ministry with ladies. She asked me if God had shown me. Tricia, I told her that before my Sunday afternoon nap, I saw myself conducting a women's seminar. Janie got all excited and said she thought God wanted her to help me with it. Maybe the three of us can work together." I finally took a breath. "Do you have an idea for a theme?"

She shook her head. "No, but I believe the Lord will show us. We need to meet and pray."

"Good idea." I said. "When and where?"

"What about Thursday. Can you come to my house at 2 o'clock in the afternoon?"

I liked Tricia. Like Janie, she was very decisive. I needed friends who could make quick decisions.

"We'll go to my 'prayer chamber'," she continued, "I have a white fur rug on the floor and a small sofa facing the upstairs fireplace. It's a perfect place to pray."

"I'll be there."

Houses have always fascinated me. I loved visiting my friend's homes and looked forward to seeing Tricia's beautiful two story house again. It sat in a small tangle of woods that made a country setting, yet it was in the city of Jacksonville, Florida. I had not yet visited her *prayer chamber* as she called it and was anxious to see it.

Tricia had recently learned more about the value of prayer. She started by setting aside her lunch hour every Tuesday to pray for her brother. He had many problems she desired to see solved. That hour of prayer became so exciting to her that she wanted to expand her knowledge of the subject. Her husband's grandmother, Granny Jumpp, loaned her several books. After devouring them, prayer was now her favorite topic.

Thursday came and I rang Tricia's doorbell. She welcomed me in and we trod up the stairs to her prayer chamber. I admired it for a few minutes before we prayed. We had barely entered the throne room of God when we knew the subject for our seminar was spiritual warfare and the title *Women In God's Army*. I left with Tricia telling me that the rest would come. By the next day, I knew who God wanted to speak and I knew their subject. Within minutes I had it all on paper. It involved four women instead of three.

WOMEN IN GOD'S ARMY CONFERENCE

Tricia Jumpp spoke first, her subject - *The Women*. Ladies needed to know about the women who fight in this spiritual battle. Who are they? Tricia told us and gave us a bonus of comedy as she illustrated those in the Bible and modern women.

When Tricia was twelve-years-old she felt the call of God on her life to minister. Thinking it was a pulpit ministry she said to God, "No! I can't do that!" As we began the seminars, Tricia realized that *this* was the ministry God had in mind for her. She accepted her mission whole heartedly, and often commented about how fulfilled she felt after speaking at the seminars.

Later, her husband, Dale, was called to preach and Tricia spoke often as the two birthed a new church in Utah. Now Tricia has written a wonderful book entitled – *Redemption's Heritage.*

God directed me that Charlotte Pickett spoke second, her subject - *The Enemy.* Charlotte knew first-hand about the enemy's attacks. God brought her through a very bad time of divorce, deep depression, and problems with her son. I distinctly heard God say in my spirit, "It's time for Charlotte to give her testimony of what I have done in her life."

The only problem was Charlotte had never spoken in front of a group of people. By asking her to speak I was taking a chance. I could end up looking like a fool if she was not a good speaker. What if she got up and had nothing to say. I battled fear of embarrassment. Yet I couldn't get away from the idea that she was to be a part of the team.

In a few days I called her. "Charlotte," I said, "we are going to have a Ladies Seminar on *Women in God's Army.* God said that you are to be one of the speakers. You've had experiences with the enemy and God wants you to tell about it."

She laughed and said, "You're kidding, right?"

"No," I said, "I'm serious."

"I've never done anything like that. I can't stand up in front of people and talk. I wouldn't know what to say." She was still laughing.

"Yes, you can. God said that it is time for you to give your testimony. If God said it that means you can do it." I was convincing myself as I spoke.

"Are you sure?" Doubt came through from the other end of the line. Now she was dead serious.

"Yes," I said emphatically. "You can do it, Charlotte. I know you can. You have so much to tell. Besides, God said it's *time*." I emphasized time.

"Well okay." She still sounded hesitant. "If you think I can, I'll try. She drew out try." Quickly she added, "But what if I don't know what to say when I get up there?" She still wasn't convinced.

I tried to sound confident. "God will show you. You'll see. Start thinking about what God has done and write it."

"I'll try." She still didn't sound sure as she hung up the phone.

Cradling the phone I whispered, "Sure hope that was you I heard, Lord." At the first seminar, Charlotte, the woman who was afraid that she had nothing to say, spoke for over an hour. The words poured from her lips and captivated the women. During the lunch break, three people

17

went to her and said, "While you were speaking I saw a white light that circled you, outlining your body." I knew they saw the anointing of God. I *had* heard from God. The same thing happened at another church. Three people saw the outline of glory about her. Charlotte was the favorite speaker for many women at the seminars.

After lunch I spoke. My topic was *The Armor and Weapons.* God was so good to give me an illustrated sermon on the subject. I borrowed my grandson's armor. Since I am short and relatively small, (at least I was then) the child size breastplate fit. The shield, shin covers, and sword were fine too. After I bought a cardboard yet authentic looking helmet and made a girdle of truth with silver lame', I was ready to illustrate my subject.

Janie Tarpley spoke last. She was the friend who prophesied to me confirming my involvement in the seminars. I attended prayer meetings at Janie's house for seven years and received several personal prophecies there that helped me tremendously. Each week I could hardly wait for Tuesday morning.

I saw devils cast out, people healed, while others received the Holy Spirit with the evidence of speaking in tongues. An Episcopal Priest was slain in the Spirit and spoke in tongues right there on Janie's living room floor. We never knew who would come or what wonderful thing might happen.

Who knew better than Janie about the outcome of the battle? No one! Her subject was one she lived - *The Victory.*

We took the seminar across the state of Florida and even up to North Carolina. This book came from material in that seminar. I thought it bore repeating when fifteen years later a woman told me, "That seminar, *Women in God's Army,* changed my life."

My prayer is that this book will change your life, too.

Love,

Jonnie

PROTECTING YOUR HOUSE FROM PESTS

Now that your spiritual house is built, PESTS will try to invade it! We must be aware of:

WHERE they enter,

HOW they work to destroy, and

WHAT we do to rid ourselves of them.

The Bible teaches us that there is:

SPECIAL ARMOR with which to protect ourselves,

REVEALING LIGHT to expose the vermin's hiding places, and

SPIRITUAL PESTICIDE to exterminate the destroying bugs.

We must learn all we can about them to keep our spiritual house pest free. Let's get started!

PART I

WOMEN OF WAR

Finally my brethren (or sisters) be strong in the Lord, and in the power of his might (Ephesians 6:10a).

The war with pests all started with a woman - Eve in the Garden of Eden. Before she ate the forbidden fruit there were no termites to destroy, ants to torment, roaches to pollute or rats to scare. There were no flies buzzing around your ears while you tried to sleep or mosquitoes making angry itchy whelps on your skin. None of that. Life was perfect.

There was no sin, cheating, stealing or killing. Not even the thought of doing wrong was in Adam and Eve's mind - that is, not until God said, "DO NOT." He told them that they could eat of all the trees in the garden EXCEPT one. He said, "DO NOT eat from the tree of the knowledge of good and evil."

Why do we want to do what we are told not to do? God had provided such wonderful provisions for them. They had all the herbs of the field and a great variety of fruit to eat from many different trees. God is so good to provide for us all that we need and in various flavors. He did not make life boring with only one type of food. He provides much for us today also, but we, like the first couple are not satisfied with what God supplies. We want the thing that God says *do not touch.*

Eve ate the fruit that God forbade and offered it to her husband, Adam. He ate also and everything bad entered into a perfect world: sin, sickness, disease, decay, sorrow, grief, pain, murder, separation, old age and death. Because Adam and Eve sinned, all women suffer the consequences. Men, too.

Disobedience to God still creates the same effect. He wants our lives to be blessed, but we say *no* to His rules and the *destroying pests* enter. They make our life miserable. We influence others to do wrong just as Eve influenced Adam and the cycle continues.

Is there hope for change so that we don't keep sinning and influencing others thus tearing down our house instead of building it up?

Yes, there is! Though Eve was a bad example and disobeyed still there were many strong, Godly women in the Bible who set a good example for us to follow.

(For an example read *Wives of the Bible* by Jonnie Whittington, Pathway Press, publisher.)

EXAMPLES OF STRONG WOMEN IN THE BIBLE

RUTH, A WILLING WORKER, was not raised to know the true God. She lived in Moab where they worshiped Chemosh. Believing a falsehood, Moabites threw their children into the fire as a sacrifice to this fake god.

Ruth married Naomi's son, Mahlon, an Israelite who with his father, mother, and brother had moved to Moab because of a famine in Israel. Mahlon and his family worshiped Jehovah. When he, his brother Chilion, and his father Elimelech all died, Ruth chose to follow Naomi, her mother-in-law, back to Israel. She proclaimed before leaving, "Your people shall be my people and your God my God."

After arriving in Israel, Ruth took care of her mother-in-law, Naomi. She gleaned barley in the fields to provide food. Hot, backbreaking work, she followed the reapers and picked up sheaves they dropped. Ruth worked cheerfully and out of a heart of love for Naomi. In turn, God provided her with a new, wealthy husband. She and Naomi never lacked for anything again.

Ruth was a strong woman willing to work hard. Are you willing to work for the things that you need? There are plenty of jobs in America. Anyone who desires to be successful in business can be, by putting God's laws into practice and hard work.

If you are handicapped God will provide something within your reach, something that you are capable of doing. Trust Him and be willing. Cultivate a cheerful attitude. Your life depends much on your attitude and work ethics. Nobody owes you anything. You are responsible for yourself. Ouch, that hurts, doesn't it? You and I come from the *I deserve it*, age.

NAOMI, AN INFLUENTIAL MOTHER-IN-LAW, grew up knowing about Jehovah, and taught her daughter-in-law, Ruth about the one true God. Ruth saw something in Naomi that she desired to pattern after. Something she wanted so much that she was willing to change her whole life and leave her old ways behind. What a difference the influence of Naomi made on Ruth.

It doesn't matter if you were raised to be a Christian, like Naomi or a heathen like Ruth, you can come to Jesus Christ the son of Jehovah and He will change your life.

Read about both strong women in the Old Testament of the Bible in the book of Ruth.

ESTHER, THE ORPHAN, became a queen. With both parents dead, you might think that Esther would be bitter and resentful blaming God for the loss of her parents. You might think that she didn't have a chance in life without a father and mother to teach her about important things. But God had a plan. Her older cousin, Mordeciah, took her to his house and raised her to know God.

No matter your circumstances in life God has other plans for you. Good plans!

Ahasuerus, king of one hundred and twenty seven provinces from India to Ethiopia, sought a new queen. Who would ever think that an orphan girl could fill that bill? But Esther did. The king selected her out of many beautiful women from all over the provinces and crowned her queen. In that position, Esther risked her life to save her people, the Jews.

Our beginning in life, who our parents are (we have no control over that) or whether we have parents is not important to God. He has a purpose for us and can turn our life around for good.

Read Esther, the orphan's heroic story in the book of Esther.

DEBORAH, A PROPHETESS, was the judge of Israel. Highly regarded as a woman of God, Deborah prophesied that God would give Israel the victory in battle against Jabin, king of Canaan. Ba'rak, Israel's military leader, was afraid to go to war without this woman of God in his chariot. When he insisted, she warned him that he would not get credit for this victory, but it would go to a woman.

Deborah became known as *the Mother of Israel.*

Are you willing to allow God to give others a word of encouragement through you as Deborah did to Ba'rak? Will you hold a position in the government as a judge like Deborah?

Read about this strong prophetess and judge in the fourth and fifth chapters of the book of Judges.

ABIGAII, THE PEACEMAKER, made up for the evil of her drunken husband, Nabal.

David's troop had protected Nabal's sheep and herders. In return Nabal refused to feed these men. David was on his way to kill Nabal's entire household. When Abigail got wind of the situation, she loaded up ample food supplies on donkeys, mounted her horse and carried it to the troops herself. As she met David, she dismounted and bowed to the ground. She spoke words of encouragement to him and apologized for not knowing the situation sooner. David's wrath dissipated and he changed his mind about killing her people thanking her for stopping him from doing this great evil.

In a few days, Abigail's husband died and King David married her. She went from being the wife of a stingy drunken man to the wife of a king.

If you are serving Satan you are in a similar situation. Satan is your master. He is stingy and evil. You can put him out of your life and accept Jesus as Lord. He is the King of glory! That makes you His queen!

Are you in a difficult marriage? Be strong and keep a good attitude. Do the right thing in all circumstances. Abigail did.

Find her story in I Samuel chapters 25-30.

SARAH, RESPECTFUL AND BEAUTIFUL, was married to Abraham, the richest man of his day. Sarah honored her husband calling him Lord. Though she was obedient and beautiful, Sarah was unable to have children. God promised her and Abraham a son who would bless the world. After many years of waiting, trying to work things out and failing, finally, when she was ninety years old, she gave birth to her son, Isaac. He is in the lineage of Jesus, the greatest blessing known to mankind.

Pray, be patient and wait on God's promises, a little longer as Sarah did. God always comes through, and is never late.

Sarah's story is interspersed between chapters 12

and 23 of Genesis.

KING LEMUEL'S MOTHER, A TEACHER OF TRUTH, in Proverbs chapter thirty one, advises her son about women and drink. In verses 10-31 of the same chapter she describes the perfect wife - the virtuous woman:

She arose before day to provide breakfast for her family. Making sure they had warm clothing in winter, she wove the fabric and created their clothes. Her house was clean and comfortable with beautiful tapestry. A business woman, she sewed garments and sold them to the merchants. With the money, she bought property and planted a vineyard. Never idle, she stayed up late at night to get her work done. She made sure that her household ran smoothly. She was kind to the poor and needy and offered words of wisdom and kindness. Her husband and children praised her for all of her good work.

This woman's husband was successful. The Bible says that he was known in the gate where he sat among the elders. That means he was a man of importance in the city. The legal proceedings were carried out in a large room built on the city gate.

When I worked for Home Interiors and Gifts, I learned that most successful men come from well decorated homes.

Do you take care of your children and husband? If so, one day they will brag on you. If it hasn't happened yet, just keep looking after them and know that God's Word is true. They will *arise and call you blessed.*

LYDIA, A BUSINESS WOMAN, sold purple fabric. One day she heard the Apostle Paul preach. Believing his words, she accepted Jesus and worshiped God. Her whole household came to the Lord, too and were baptized. She provided a room for Paul and Silas during their stay in Thyatira.

Her story is in the New Testament in the book of Acts 16:14-15, 40.

PRISCILLA, A TENTMAKER AND TEACHER ABOUT JESUS CHRIST, worked beside her husband Aquila. They met Paul who was in the same business and traveled to Ephesus with him. Apollos, a man of that city, only knew about John's Baptism unto repentance. Priscilla, with her husband Aquila, took Apollos aside and taught him the true way of Jesus. They started a church in their home.

Some women work with their husband both in the business world and as ministers of the Word of God. I worked as a partner in ministry with my husband for 50 years. We shared responsibilities both at home and in the church.

At home he loved to cook. I didn't, so he did most of that. He hated to do dishes so I did all of them. At church I loved teaching so he allowed me to teach Bible classes. He was an excellent preacher and did most of that. I sang and played keyboard and taught piano so the music was my job. He handled business and was very responsible thus he was in charge of that area. Together we made quite a ministry team just as Aquila and Priscilla.

God may have a wonderful partner for you. Will you ask Him and then wait for Him to provide the right person in your life?

Read about Priscilla in Acts 18:2-3, 26. Romans 16:3 and I Corinthians 16:19.

DORCAS, A SEAMSTRESS AND DISCIPLE, was a wonderful woman who sewed garments and gave them to widows and needy. People commended her for all her good deeds and her giving. Dorcas died. The people mourned and talked about her wonderful works showing Peter the garments she had made for others. Peter put all of the mourners out of the room and prayed. He spoke to the dead body to arise and took her hand. Life returned and Dorcus arose from the dead.

Read her miraculous story in Acts 9:36, 39.

STRONG WOMEN OF TODAY

You have read the Biblical account of ten strong and godly women. There are many more. I'm sure you can think of others that you have read about. Likewise, today many women are doing great things for God.

I have read about Corrie Ten Boon, Sister Teresa, Aimee Simple McPherson, Marie Woodworth Etter, Kathryn Kuhlman, Ruth Graham.

I have seen on television, Marilyn Hickey, Gloria Copeland, Joyce Meyer and other godly women.

Listed are Church of God women who come to mind:

Annette Watson began evangelizing at the age of sixteen. She has preached at the Church of God General Assembly and ministered to thousands throughout the world in women's services, banquets and seminars.

Marilyn Weeks began to evangelize after her husband pastor died. She is a blessing to many.

Margaret Kirby, a pastor of a church on our district, was loved and respected by the community.

Bonnie Brannen ministered to me when I was a teenager. I still remember the scripture she helped me memorize in a service and the sermon she preached.

Amanda Miller – I was fifteen when I heard her preach and was slain in the Spirit for the first time.

Marion Spellman, with her husband's support, started a drug rehab in Pennsylvania where many have gained freedom from drugs and alcohol.

Lesa Henderson, a friend who was our main speaker in the Set Free meetings God led me to start, and later she headed our Women Warriors of God conferences. She was a mighty influence in my life with prophecies from God.

Shelisa Hull another prophetess who spoke many encouraging words of prophecy to me.

You could add to the list of women who have made or are making a difference in people's lives. No doubt you have been helped and influenced by one or more of God's mighty women.

WILL YOU BE A STRONG WOMAN FOR GOD?

Like these women, you too can be a strong woman. God intends for you to be mighty. He has everything you need to help you be the woman He created you to be. Do you believe that? He is for you. He loves you with an everlasting love. He is good all the time and has your best interest at heart. Be strong. Be encouraged. He has provided you with the equipment to fight this spiritual battle and win!

In order to be all that God created you to be, you must accept God's son, Jesus. He died on the cross for the sins that fell on us because Adam and Eve disobeyed. When you confess that you have sinned and ask God to forgive you, He will. He comes into your life and changes your nature. He washes away the evil that was forced on you when sin entered into the world and the sin that you willfully committed after you were old enough to make the choice to do wrong.

TO BE A STRONG WOMAN FOR GOD, ONE MUST ACCEPT HIS SON JESUS CHRIST

If you are sorry for your sins pray with me,

Dear God,

I desire to be the woman that You created me to be. I cannot change without Your help. Just as Adam and Eve disobeyed and ate the forbidden fruit I too disregarded Your laws. I'm sorry for each time I defied you by not keeping Your commandments. Please forgive and take away all the sin in my life. Forgive my rebellion against

You.

Please strengthen me to be all You want me to be. Make me a warrior against the pests that have invaded my life.

I desire to be a woman who helps others. Let me be an example of right living to my family and friends.

In Jesus' name I pray. Amen.

PESTICIDE

Answer these questions and begin the process of getting rid of the pests in your life.

What kind of evil entered your life because Adam and Eve sinned? We don't get rid of things until we acknowledge them. List the sins that you have committed and for which you are sorry. Nobody sees them, but you and God.

_____

_____

What have you lost because of these sins?

_____

_____

Name all of the good women in the Bible you remember.

_____

_____

Read the Bible account of several women. What did they do to help?

_____

_____

Name modern day women who have made a difference in others._____

_____

Select a book from the library about one of them. Read it.

Who is or was a Godly example to you?

_____

Will you be one who helps others by living a pure life?

You can be a strong woman in the Lord and fight to rid your house of spiritual pests.

PART II

THE ENEMY

Women Dressed for War

"Eight people are dead!" the woman said. "Five have been taken to the hospital!" The woman stood on the other side of the counter in the Parking Division at City Hall in downtown Jacksonville, Florida. She had come to pay a parking fine. I heard her from my desk. "The man was crazy! He walked into the GMAC office building right here in Jacksonville and started shooting. Nobody knows why. He has killed all those innocent people!" Her voice held a sob.

After she left a co-worker and I discussed the incident. We thought of how horrible it was for the families! Immediately I wondered about the eight people who died, *where are they right now? Are their souls in heaven or hell?*

The other girl was thinking about our own vulnerability, how that as office workers in a public building anyone who decided to do it, could come in and gun us down. There were eight employees in our office. That could have been us. She turned in her chair to face me and said, "My God, we are in a war!"

How true for the Christian, I thought. The only difference is that our warfare is not against flesh and blood. Our warfare is against demons and devils and Satan himself. Immediately the scripture came to mind. *For we wrestle not against flesh and blood, but against principalities, against powers, against the rulers of the darkness of this world, against spiritual wickedness in high places (Ephesians 6:12).*

Yes, we have an enemy and we are in a war, but our war is not with people. The person that you think is your enemy - is not. We fight against another person thinking he is the true enemy. Your enemy is not your husband or your boss. Your enemy is not the one who cheated you or hit you. Your enemy is not the one who stole your stuff. Your enemy is not the attacker or rapist. Your enemy is Satan.

We have misunderstood too long. We thought that we had to fight people. Even in churches people war against each other. Can't we band together and fight the true enemy. There is strength in numbers. The Bible teaches that one can put a thousand to flight but two can put ten thousand to flight. Two people can accomplish ten times as much as one. Join forces with your husband against the enemy instead of fighting him. Don't you see that Satan tries to divide you to keep you from accomplishing your goals and dreams? Join forces. Be on the same team. Fight the true enemy – Satan.

Satan has wrecked our homes, stolen our children, taken away our goods and left us defeated. We are not going to stand for it any longer. This book is designed to transform us into spiritual warriors by teaching us to don the armor of God and pick up our weapons.

Prepare for battle! Get ready to fight! We are going to war!

PART II

THE ENEMY

Put on the whole armor of God that ye may be able to stand against the wiles of the devil.

For we wrestle not against flesh and blood, but against principalities, powers, against the rulers of the darkness of this world, against spiritual wickedness (wicked spirits) in high places (Ephesians 6:11-12).

OUR ENEMY IS NOT A PERSON

OUR ENEMY IS THE DEVIL

Be sober, be vigilant; because your adversary the devil, as a roaring lion, walketh about, seeking whom he may devour (I Peter 5:8).

The word adversary means arch enemy.

Yes, there really is a devil and he is out to get you. The Bible says that hell or everlasting fire was prepared for the devil and his angels (Matthew 25:41). He doesn't want to go there alone. He hates you and wants you in hell with him. That's why he constantly schemes and plans ways to drag you there.

HOW DID THE ENEMY GET HERE?

GOD CREATED HIM

All things were made by Him (John 1:3).

There is only one God, and he created light and darkness, peace and evil (Isaiah 45: 5-7).

For by Him (Jesus Christ) were all things created, that are in heaven, and that are in the earth, visible and invisible, whether they be thrones, or dominions, or principalities, or powers: all things were created by him, and for him. And He is before all things and by Him all things consist (Colossians 1:16-17).

Since God created all things they are subject to Him. The created is never in charge of the creator. If I construct a dress with fabric and a sewing machine I am in charge of that dress. It doesn't tell me what to do I tell it. I hang it in the closet and it stays there. We are not dresses, but God is in charge of us even though He doesn't hang us in a closet. He gave us a free will. We can choose to do what He says or we can resist.

Satan was also created by God but he chose to rebel. Still he can only do what God gives him authority to do.

Jesus Christ is gone into heaven, and is on the right hand of God; angels and authorities and powers being made subject unto him (II Peter 3:22). Satan was an angel and he is subject to God.

Ephesians 1:21-22 tells us that Jesus is over all principalities, power, might, and dominion. They are under His feet.

ENEMY NAMES

Names for the enemy are the devil, Satan and Lucifer. He was called the deceiver, evil one, the dragon, the great red dragon, the accuser of the brethren. He was also known as an arch angel. Arch means chief, ruler or leading angel. There were three arch angels in heaven. They were Michael, the warring angel, Gabriel, the bearer of good news, and Lucifer, the leader of worship and praise.

According to Ezekiel 28:11, Satan was an arch angel full of wisdom and perfect in beauty. He was in Eden, the Garden of God. He wore beautiful clothing with musical instruments built into him. Known as the chief worshipping angel and called the anointed cherub meant he led the music in heaven including praise and worship to God.

When Lucifer was cast out of heaven, he lost his job, and now hates all musicians and singers who give glory to God through their music. He is so jealous of them he can hardly stand it. That's why he tries so hard to make musicians fall away from God.

He was called anointed cherub which speaks of him as a prophet who walked in the presence of God. Satan was perfect until iniquity was found in him. When sin was born in his heart he became Satan, the devil, now the enemy of God and man.

Ezekiel describes him and compares him to the king of Tyre, Ithobalus II. Satan actually ruled and operated through the king of Tyre who claimed to be God. In the last days he will operate through the Antichrist who will also claim to be God and deceive people with lying wonders.

In the days of Daniel, the prophet, the king of Tyre became rich because of extensive trading with other nations

(Ezekiel 28:5). He believed himself wiser than Daniel because he ruled his city and organized the city fairs making lots of money.

Satan, like the king of Tyre, thought he was wiser than God. He also was lifted up with pride because of his great beauty, and assigned authority. He had tried to take over heaven but failed, he was the sole ruler of the earth before the days of Adam, but lost that position. Consequently, with great pride and cunning, he wrested it from Adam, but will someday lose it again. (Dake)

Scripture weaves back and forth between the king of Tyre and the devil describing the characteristics of each one. It seems as if God is mocking the haughty king when in Exekiel 28: 2-5, the king boasts that he is a god. But the Lord tells him, *"Yet you are a man and not a god, though you set your heart as one, (Behold, are you really wiser than Daniel?) with your wisdom and understanding you have gained riches for yourself. By your great wisdom you have increased your riches. And your heart is lifted up."* But it was never to last.

Together with other kings who claimed to be God, one day the king of Tyre would die a violent death. In the grave he would no longer claim to be greater than the God of Daniel. One day Satan will be thrown into the bottomless pit. No longer will he deceive people into believing he is more powerful than Almighty God.

EZEKIEL DESCRIBES SATAN

You were the model of perfection, full of wisdom and perfect in beauty.

You were in Eden, the garden of God; every precious stone adorned you:

Ruby, topaz and emerald, chrysolite, onyx, and jasper, sapphire, turquoise and beryl.

Your settings and mountings were made of gold; on the day you were created they were prepared.

You were anointed as a guardian cherub, for I ordained you. You were on the holy mount of God. You walked among the fiery stones.

You were blameless in your ways from the day you were created until wickedness was found in you.

So I drove you in disgrace from the mount of God, and I expelled you, O guardian cherub, from among the fiery stones.

Your heart became proud on account of your beauty, and you corrupted your wisdom because of your splendor.

So I threw you to the earth; I made a spectacle of you before kings. By your many sins and dishonest trade you have desecrated your sanctuaries.

So I made a fire come out from you and it consumed you. I reduced you to ashes on the ground in the sight of all who were watching.

All the nations who knew you are appalled at you. You have come to a horrible end and will be no more (Ezekiel 28:11-19 NIV).

ISAIAH TELLS OF SATAN'S FALL

How art thou fallen from heaven, O Lucifer, son of the morning! How art thou cut down to the ground, which didst weaken the nations!

For you have said in your heart, I will ascend into heaven. I will exalt my throne above the stars of God:

I will sit also upon the mount of the congregation, in the sides of the north: I will ascend above the heights of the clouds; I will be like the most High.

Yet you shall be brought down to hell, to the side of the pit.

They that see you shall narrowly look upon you, and consider you, saying, "Is this the man that made the earth to tremble, that did shake kingdoms;

That made the world as a wilderness, and destroyed the cities thereof; that opened not the house of his prisoners?

But you are cast out of your grave like an abominable branch, and as the raiment of those that are slain, thrust through with a sword, that go down to the stones of the pit; as a carcass trodden under feet (Isaiah 14:12-19).

JESUS SAID ABOUT SATAN

I beheld Satan as lightning fall from heaven. Behold I give unto you power to tread on serpents and scorpions, and over all the power of the enemy: and nothing shall by any means hurt you (Luke 10:18).

44

OUR ENEMY IS A DEFEATED FOE

We know this from what we have just read. Part of Isaiah and Ezekiel's words are prophecy. That means that we still have to take authority over him until he is put in the pit. Satan can take advantage of us if we are ignorant of his devices as Paul mentioned in II Corinthians. 2:11. That is the reason we are studying him.

TAKE <u>D</u> OFF OF <u>D</u>EVIL

ALL THAT'S LEFT IS <u>EVIL</u>

That describes him to a T – EVIL. When he was cast out of the third heaven where God's throne dwells, Lucifer became the devil. Devil means the accuser, the slanderer. Our enemy, the devil constantly accuses us to God. (Job 1:6-12; 2:1-7 and Revelation. 12:10).

Accuse in Greek means to hold down, to possess, and to keep (in memory).

Satan desires to hold you down and keep you back from the blessings of God. He wants to stop you in your tracks as you follow the Lord. He tells God everything he can think of to hinder you, and to possess you. But Jesus is the great intercessor who intercedes daily for you and reminds God that He paid the price for your sins.

<u>SATAN'S HELPERS:</u>

FALLEN ANGELS

Satan does not do his dirty work alone. He has helpers. When he was cast out of heaven he deceived one third of the heavenly angels and convinced them to join forces with him to try to overthrow God. They were kicked out of heaven with him and now help promote evil and fight against God.

They should have known that they could not dethrone God, yet people today still try it. They ignore His rules and think they can get by doing things their way. It will not work.

Can you imagine how Satan and the angels who followed him felt when they left the glories and beauty of heaven to roam in space? They became mad at God and are still the epitome of anger, hating God and everyone created in His image. That means that they hate you and me. Satan especially despises people who expose his schemes and minister for God.

Since the fallen angels and Satan lost fellowship with God they don't want anyone to have fellowship with Him. They know scripture says that hell was created for the devil and his angels. Not wanting to go there alone they try their best to make people turn against God, or even ignore Him, so they will go to hell with them.

Fallen angels promote the kingdom of darkness. They rule over certain areas of the world, cities, and territories promoting crime and evil. They fight against the good angels who help people, bring answers to prayer, protect children, and fulfill their mission sent on by God. The Bible shows us examples.

SATAN'S KINGDOM

Satan's kingdom is divided into four categories. They are principalities, powers, the rulers of the darkness of this world, and spiritual wickedness in high places.

PRINCIPALITIES are the chief rulers or beings of the highest rank and order in Satan's kingdom.

POWERS are those who derive their power from and execute the will of the chief rulers.

RULERS OF THE DARKNESS are the spirit world rulers.

SPIRITUAL WICKEDNESS IN HIGH PLACES are the wicked spirits or demons of Satan that live in the atmosphere above the earth called the heavenlies (Ephesians 6:12).

DEMONS

Demons are disembodied spirits who try to possess a human body or an animal in order to operate. They possess a person through a door that the human opens. Later we will discuss some of these openings so that we are aware of how they take possession. If we do not know how they get in we lose control.

Demons also try to influence people, even Christians. Don't you want to be aware of how they work so that you can guard against their evil influences? Remember we don't want to be ignorant of Satan's wiles - plans and devices.

The word demon is not found in the King James Version of the Bible. However, the word evil spirit and devil are both translated from the original Greek to mean demon. The English word devil has three different Greek words. One is diabolos and means Satan, the prince of demons. He is the chief devil and original source of evil in the universe, the chief adversary of God.

In other places of the Bible where devil or devils are used, the two Greek words are diamonion, and diamon. They both mean evil spirits or devils. We call them demons. There is only one prince of devils but many demons.

Other names the Bible uses for demons are familiar spirits, unclean spirits, and evil spirits, seducing spirits, and spirits of infirmity. Whatever they are called they are evil and cause much havoc, pain, sorrow, suffering, confusion, sickness, division, and anything else that's wrong.

SIGNS OF DEMON ACTIVITY

BLINDNESS

Matthew 12:22 tells us that demons cause blindness and dumbness. Matthew said, "a man was brought to Jesus one possessed with a devil, blind, and dumb; and Jesus healed him, so that the blind and dumb both spake and saw." That's pretty plain that a devil or in the Greek language a demon caused the problem. When Jesus healed him the demon left and the man could do things that were impossible before.

DEAF, DUMB, CONVULSIONS, AND SUICIDAL

In Mark 9:17, a father brought his son, who could not hear or speak, to Jesus. The son was demon possessed. The Bible describes him of having convulsions when the demon threw him into the fire and water trying to kill him. In verse 25 Jesus said, "Thou dumb and deaf spirit, I charge thee, come out of him, and enter no more into him."

The spirit cried out and tried to tear the boy when he came out. The boy fell to the ground as though dead. Jesus took him by the hand and helped him up. Matthew 17:18 tells about the same boy. He said, "Jesus rebuked the devil and he departed out of him and the child was cured from that very hour." When the spirit left, the boy was normal.

LUNACY AND MANIA

The man described in Mark 5:1-18 had an unclean spirit which caused a number of maladies. First he was out of his mind proven by the fact that he lived in a cemetery. A person would have to be insane to live there. No normal person chooses to live among the tombs.

Next, the Bible infers that he refused to wear his clothes going stark naked. That's just not normal, but another sign of demon activity. All people who want to go naked may not be demon possessed as this man, but they are influenced by demons.

When Adam and Eve first sinned they realized they were naked because the glory of God that had been their covering was no longer there. They tried to cover their body with fig leaves. God wanted more than that. He killed an animal, took the skin and made a coat for them to hide their naked body. Since then, it is His plan that people wear clothes. Demons try to influence you not to wear them.

Years ago when my husband was a child he had an uncle who lost his mind about once a year. When it happened he ripped off his clothes and ran down the road like a wild man. The authorities came each time with a strait jacket and took him to a mental ward for treatment. When he returned to his right mind he wore his clothes and was peaceful. It is sad that they didn't know that he could be delivered.

You may wonder, why the medicine helped if it was demons. I wondered that myself until a child at a school where I worked said to me, "Demons hate that medicine." He referred to medicine that balanced the brain chemistry which he had to take. "They hate it and leave when you take it." He said it with a calm assurance.

"Have you seen them?" I asked.

He nodded then hurried from the office. I had the impression that he didn't want to be questioned about his experience. If medicine makes demons leave surely we women of God can take authority over them

In the Bible, when the demons left the man, Jesus said, *He was sitting, clothed, and in his right mind (Mark 5:15).*

SUPERNATURAL STRENGTH

The third sign of demon possession in this man in the Bible is supernatural strength. Many times men tried to control him and bound him with chains and fetters. We know what chains are but may not understand the word fetters. It means shackles for the feet. Every time the restraints were put on him with inhuman strength he tore them off.

Satan didn't want him controlled. He couldn't hurt himself or others when he was bound. Sometimes we need restraints. Many women told me during my jail ministry that God allowed them to go to jail where they are controlled to save their life. They needed help to manage themselves. In jail they could not get the drugs or alcohol that was destroying their lives.

If we put Jesus in charge of our lives, He can give us the desire to overcome problems and gain self-control to function in society.

Parents need to teach their children about self-control so that as they mature the devil doesn't control them.

SELF INFLICTED PAIN

The fourth sign of demons in this man in the Bible was that he cut himself with stones. Self infliction is a sign of demon activity. I have known women who burned themselves with cigarette butts, cut their arms with razors, and scratched their neck with their fingernails till they bled to inflict pain. They said that they hurt so badly within from neglect or sexual abuse from their fathers or others, that they thought if they hurt their body they wouldn't feel the pain inside. That is a lie from demons. You don't have to hurt yourself.

If that has happened to you and you now inflict pain on your body, stop! Bring your inward pain to Jesus. He can heal your hurt. The demon that influences you to hurt yourself will have to leave if you command it to go in the name of Jesus. All demons are subject to people who confess their sins, forsake them, forgive everyone who has hurt them and love Jesus with all their heart. They don't have to be tormented by them any longer.

DEMONS BOW BEFORE JESUS

As soon as the man saw Jesus the demons in him caused him to run, fall down and worship Him. Demons know that Jesus is Lord and that every knee shall bow before Him. They were with Him in heaven before their fall.

They immediately used the man's voice and cried out to Jesus saying, "What have I to do with thee, Jesus, thou Son of the most high God? I adjure thee by God, that thou torment me not." For Jesus had said unto him, "Come out of the man, thou unclean spirit." Then Jesus asked him his name. He answered through the man's voice, "Legion, for we are many."

The demons understood that they had to obey Jesus. They begged Jesus not to send them out of the country but to let them go into a herd of two thousand swine that were feeding nearby. He gave them permission. They went into the swine driving the pigs mad so that they ran into the lake and drowned themselves. This makes me think that demons cause suicide. If you know someone that is suicidal, bind that spirit. You don't have to touch the person or even let them know until God directs you to talk to them.

When the demons left, the man was free. He wanted to follow Jesus everywhere he went, but Jesus told him, "Go home to thy friends, and tell them how great things the Lord hath done for thee, and hath had compassion on thee." The man did as Jesus said, and people marveled at his wonderful change.

SICKNESS, DISEASE, AND TORMENTS

Jesus healed all the people brought to him (Matthew 4:23-24). They had many things wrong with them. Some were demon possessed others afflicted by demons. I believe that all sickness is caused by demons. That does not mean that a sick person is possessed. It means that they are attacked by them. Sickness is not from God. There is no sickness in heaven therefore it is not God's will for people to be sick. He said to pray, *Thy will be done on earth as it is in heaven.* I want to be well on earth as I will be well in heaven.

How God anointed Jesus of Nazareth with the Holy Ghost and with power; who went about doing good, and healing all that were oppressed of the devil; for God was with him (Acts 10:38).

That said to me that sickness is an oppression of the devil, because Jesus healed everyone who came to Him. Never one time did He say, "This sickness is from God. I

53

won't heal it". No! He healed EVERY SICK PERSON that came to Him.

I know that our lifestyle and diet plays a big role in our health. But it is Satan's plan to keep us from eating a healthy diet and living a clean lifestyle. We often open the door to demon activity by the things we do and eat. God provides guidelines in the Bible of how to live and the proper diet. If we stick with His program Satan's demons have to stay out of our life. When we are sick, it doesn't necessarily mean that we have sinned. We may be ignorant of the right things to do. God said in the Scripture, *My people are destroyed for a lack of knowledge.* We can read the Bible and know both, what to eat, and what not to eat, and how to live our lives.

NO ONE'S SIN CAUSED THIS SICKNESS

Jesus saw a man who was born blind. His disciples asked him who had sinned, the man or his parents. "Neither," Jesus answered, "but that the works of God should be made manifest in him (John 9:1-3).

God likes to undo what Satan does to a person.

DID THIS MAN'S SINS CAUSE HIS SICKNESS?

In another account in John 5:1-14, Jesus insinuated that a man was sick because of sin. The man lay by the pool of Bethesda with many other sick people. At a certain season, an angel came down and troubled the water. Whoever got into the water first was healed. This man had no one to help him into the pool. He had been sick for thirty eight years.

Jesus, full of compassion, healed him. Then he warned, *Go and sin no more lest a worse thing come upon you.* Sin can and does cause certain sicknesses. Repent of the sin and ask God to heal. He never turned anyone away in the Bible.

FALSE DOCTRINES

In the latter days people will depart from the true faith by listening to seducing spirits and doctrines of devils (I Timothy 4:1).

Yes, demons do spread false doctrines and religions. I am appalled at the false religions in America. This country was founded by Christians to be a Christian nation. The pilgrims came here to be free to worship the true God, through Jesus Christ. Now our freedom is in jeopardy. School children are not allowed to sing about the birth of Jesus at Christmas time. Officials want to call it a holiday instead of Christmas because Christ is part of the name.

We have listened to demons until we are confused about separation of church and state. Our government was founded by men who honored Christ and celebrated His birth in the office buildings at the Capitol of our country. They never intended for Christ to be taken out of Christmas, school, or government.

Try the spirits and see if they are of God because many false prophets are gone out into the world (I John 4:1-6). We can tell if a person is of God by what they confess about Jesus. If they deny Him then they are not of God. They are from a spirit of error - a demon.

COUNTERFEIT WORSHIP

And they shall no more offer their sacrifices unto devils (demons) after whom they have gone a whoring (Leviticus 17:7).

They sacrificed unto devils, not to God (Deuteronomy 32:17).

And he (Jeroboam) ordained him priests for the high places, and for the devils, and for the calves which he had made (II Chronicles 11:15).

Yea, they sacrificed their sons and daughters unto devils (Ps 106:37).

But I say that the things which the Gentiles sacrifice, they sacrifice to devils, and not to God: and I would not that ye should have fellowship with devils (I Corinthians 10:20).

And the rest of the men which were not killed by these plagues yet repented not of the works of their hands, that they should not worship devils, and idols of gold, and silver and brass, and stone, and of wood: which neither can see, nor hear, nor walk, neither repented they of their murders, nor of their sorceries, nor of their fornications, nor of their thefts (Revelation 9:20).

These Scriptures depict false worship. Any worship that is not to the true God is worship of demons. All worship of statues is worship of demons. Yet people in America put them in their homes for decoration. That's inviting in demons.

The people in the Old Testament burned their children in the fire thus offering them to idols. God was very displeased with this and said they were offering them to devils or demons. Let's worship Jesus, the true God.

When I served in jail ministry in Orlando, one night a girl gave me her testimony. She was raised in another country and taught to worship snakes. As a child she did it in obedience to her parents. She didn't know why they worshipped them.

When she and her husband came to America, her husband became addicted to drugs. He made life miserable for her. He beat her every day until she thought she would die. People who worship demons don't know how to show love because they have no love, but those who worship Jesus are good and loving to their companion.

This woman showed me a picture of her four sons. They were beautiful boys who were well behaved and made excellent grades in school. She loved them and wanted a good life for them.

One day, authorities came to arrest her husband for selling drugs, but he lied and convinced them that it was his wife who dealt the drugs. They arrested her and sent her to jail and left the drug addict husband at home.

She was confused and sad and missed her sons. She felt like her life was over. Then she saw a Bible in the jail and began to read. She learned about a God who loved her so much that He gave His Son to die for her sins.

She decided that He was the true God and she wanted Him to be her God. She repented of her sins, accepted Him as her savior and fell in love with Jesus. She said that when they falsely arrested her and put her in jail, the true God had rescued her from being beat to death by her husband. Several times she repeated, "God is so awesome!"

When we prayed together, she began to speak in tongues. After prayer, I asked if she knew what was happening. She said no, but that she prayed like that a lot in private and didn't know what she was saying. I told her that was the Holy Spirit praying through her and gave her Scriptures to read for further enlightenment.

Thank God, He brought this woman from counterfeit worship of snakes to worship of the true God, Jesus Christ.

ENCHANTMENTS AND WITCHCRAFT

And he caused his children to pass through the fire in the valley of the son of Hinnom: also he observed times, and used enchantments, and used witchcraft and dealt with a familiar spirit, and with wizards: he wrought much evil in the sight of the Lord, to provoke him to anger (II Chronicles 33:6).

False worship goes along with witchcraft which is from demons. That includes: fortune tellers, palm readers, tarot cards, séances, Ouija boards, horoscope, Voodoo, spells, incantations, demonic books such as Harry Potter, demonic games such as Dungeons and Dragons, demonic movies such as The Exorcist, etc.

The Greek word for witchcraft in the New Testament is pharmakeia from which we get the word pharmacy. It comes from a word that means medication or spell giving potion, a druggist, or poisoner, a magician or sorcerer. It means magic, sorcery, witchcraft.

If we have been involved with any of the above things that have to do with witchcraft, we should denounce it, turn from it; and burn books or other items that have anything to do with witchcraft. Then command the evil spirits to leave. That will close the door to demons that came as a result of our involvement.

The graven images of their gods shall ye burn with fire: thou shalt not desire the silver or gold that is on them, nor take it unto thee, lest thou be snared therein; for it is an abomination to the Lord thy God.

Neither shalt thou bring an abomination into thine house, lest thou be a cursed thing like it: but thou shalt utterly detest it, and thou shalt utterly abhor it; for it is a cursed thing (Deuteronomy 7:25 – 26).

Get rid of anything that could bring a curse on your house. You don't need that.

King Saul in I Samuel 15, did not obey God and leave the enemy's plunder. He saved the best cattle and sheep pretending that he wanted to offer the animals to God. But God said that disobedience or rebellion is as the sin of witchcraft. God did not want the things that idolaters owned. He knew that evil spirits hang around those things. He wanted them destroyed.

FEAR

There are several types of fear mentioned in the Bible. First, it says to fear God. That word in Greek is Phobeo which means to be in awe, revere, be afraid or reverence. When we realize that God has all power and can do anything, it creates a reverential fear in us for Him. That is a good thing.

God has not given us a spirit of fear (II Timothy 1:7). This word for fear in Greek is deilia and means timidity. Deilia is derived from another word failos and means faithless or fearful. The rest of the Scripture tells us that God has given us power, love and a sound mind. He doesn't want us to be timid because of a lack of faith, but bold.

There is no fear in love; but perfect love casts out fear: because fear hath torment. He that feareth is not made perfect in love (I John 4:18). The Greek word for this fear is Phobos which means: alarm or fright, be afraid exceedingly, terror. When you love God with a pure heart, that love will cast out the demon of fear that caused you to be terrified and tormented. Jesus said if you love me keep my commandments. He said all the commandments are summed up in this, love God with all your heart, strength and mind and love your neighbor as yourself. Do you love in that capacity? If so, fear has to go.

My friend Janie told of a nineteen-year-old college girl who came to her prayer meeting, became born again, and received the Holy Spirit. The girl asked Janie to pray about her nightmares that occurred regularly. Janie began to command the spirit of nightmare, which had caused all of this fear, to go.

A demon spoke and said they would not leave because they had been there for years, the girl was their territory and they were staying. Janie battled for about two hours telling the demons they had no more authority over this girl because she had accepted Jesus and served Him now and they had to go in the name of Jesus. At one point the demons threw the girl down and put her in an unconscious state. She looked dead. Finally in exhaustion Janie asked the Holy Spirit to saturate the girl's body and drive the demons out.

The girl came to and said, "Oh, they're leaving; it's frogs, . . . lizards, . . . leaches, and creepy crawling things." In a few moments the girl's writhing stopped her face flooded with light and peace.

When she got up off the floor, Janie asked her when those demons entered her. She said, "When I was about three years old my parents took me to a scary movie. In it were frogs, and lizards, and leaches, and creepy crawling things. I was terrified. After that night I had nightmares and have never slept without a light.

Parents, guard what your children see in movies and over the internet. Fear, trauma and accidents that a person has no control over can open a door for demons as it had in this girl's life.

After her deliverance, that girl had a wonderful vision of heaven. She was no longer afraid and had no more nightmares.

BONDAGE

For ye have not received the spirit of bondage (slavery) again to fear, (Phobos) but ye have received the Spirit of adoption, whereby we cry, Abba Father. The Spirit itself beareth witness with our spirit, that we are the children of God (Romans 8:15).

You don't have to be in bondage any longer. Once you repent of your sins and accept Jesus as your Lord, you are adopted into the family of God. He gives you authority over all spirits. You can command demons of bondage to go and they have to leave. Don't let drugs or alcohol or any other habit control you. You can take control over them and live free in the name of Jesus.

I have witnessed women in jail set free of drug addiction. I treasure a letter received from a former inmate. She wrote two years after leaving the jail to thank me and my partners, Chris and Mary, for going as volunteers to hold services every Tuesday evening. We had to drive over an hour each way in heavy traffic to get there.

I remembered the night the girl was delivered from crack cocaine. After prayer she threw up in the trash can. She told us that her father started her on drugs at eight-years-old when he gave her marijuana. She graduated to cocaine and had smoked it since a teen. After her deliverance and release from jail, she went to a new town, found a church to attend, met and married a wonderful man, and became the manager of a restaurant. It had been two years and she was still drug free.

We received other thanks for our prayers of deliverance, but this one girl's card made the six years of Tuesday night trips worth it.

Don't stay in bondage. You too can be free.

MURDER and JEALOUSY

At times, these two spirits work together. We see that in the life of King Saul.

But the Spirit of the Lord departed from Saul, and an evil spirit from the Lord troubled him (II Samuel 16:14).

King Saul disobeyed God and inquired of a witch. God's Spirit left him and this Scripture says that an evil spirit troubled him. After a battle he heard the women of Israel singing a song that attributed more glory to David than to the king. They sang that Saul killed his thousands, but David killed his ten thousands.

Saul became jealous and threw his javelin at David to kill him. When he missed, he took his army and chased David determined to murder him. We know that God had other plans for David and spared his life. We never read that Saul repented and was delivered of the evil spirit though at times, when David played his harp, the spirit left him

DELIVERED OF MURDER AND JEALOUSY

A new woman came to Janie's prayer meeting. We'll call her Mrs. Doe to protect her identity. Janie asked if she could pray for her. Mrs. Doe said yes, and Janie began to cast out demons that the Lord had already revealed to her.

Every time she cast one out the evil spirit made a sound that imitated the name of the spirit. For instance, when she told self pity to go Mrs. Doe wrinkled her face, poked out her bottom lip and made a whimpering noise like one feeling sorry for oneself.

I had just begun attending the prayer meetings and wondered if Mrs. Doe was just making the noises and how she could make them sound so realistic.

When Janie commanded a spirit of murder to leave I was shocked and thought, *this woman wouldn't hurt a flea much less murder another human being,* until Mrs. Doe's face contorted and she let out a blood curdling scream that sounded exactly like a person killing someone.

The sound gave me cold chills.

Janie sensed my fear and said quickly. "Devil, don't you think you're going to scare any of us. We have power over you in the name of Jesus and we are not afraid." My fear immediately subsided.

Janie cast out several more spirits and Mrs. Doe's face broke into a radiant smile. We knew that she was free.

Mrs. Doe left the meeting and got into the car with the woman who brought her. She opened her purse, and pulled out a gun. She said, "Here take this. I don't need it anymore. When I got home, I was going to kill my husband."

I never again doubted anyone's deliverance in those meetings.

What surprises me even as I write is that jealousy accompanied murder in Saul and in this woman. She was going to murder her husband because he had been unfaithful to her.

I WAS DELIVERED

Tormented by jealousy, I never felt any inclination toward murder.

I was saved at eight-years-old and received the Holy Spirit and spoke in tongues at nine-years-old. My husband had been a pastor for at least five years when I was attacked by a spirit of jealousy. I had begun to watch a soap opera every day in which someone was constantly running around with someone else's husband or wife.

I was not tempted to be unfaithful to my husband, but believed that a woman in the church wanted my husband. He never did anything to cause the jealousy, but I thought she did. It was the activity of a jealous spirit that tormented me. The Bible says that jealousy is as cruel as the grave and I found that to be true. I fussed at my husband for things the woman did or said and made life miserable for both of us.

One night when I felt I couldn't stand the stress any longer, I fell to my knees, sobbing and begging God to show me what was wrong with me that made me so unhappy. I went to bed and was almost asleep when I heard the television click on at the foot of our bed. I lifted my head expecting to see it lit and saw that it was still dark. In my spirit God said, "That's your problem. The soap opera you watch every day is affecting your thinking."

I said to God, "Oh Lord, I love watching that soap. You know I don't want the kids to say anything, make a noise or the phone to ring while it's on. I don't think I can give it up, but if you will do it for me I'm willing. I must have your help."

I drifted off to sleep. When I awoke the next morning, I had no desire to ever see a soap opera again. Deliverance had come and I could deal with the jealousy.

Several years later in a different church and without watching a soap opera, I became extremely jealous again with a different woman. The torment was back. I accused my husband of talking longer with that woman than others in the church. I harped and griped. It made a strain on him. He didn't know whether to speak to her or not when he went to church and he didn't dare lay hands on her head if she came up for prayer. I was so miserable it was unbearable.

One night during a revival at another church in town, I went up for prayer, not really knowing why I was there. E. L. Terry was the evangelist. He prayed for everyone else through the microphone, but when he started to pray for me he put the microphone down and spoke in my ear where no one else could hear, "Sister, I see that you find it hard to forgive and have resentment."

He's talking about my mother. I always thought that was a problem with her, but couldn't see it in myself. How we like to shovel God's words to us on to someone else. His next words stopped me in my track. He said, "And at times you have more than a normal amount of jealousy."

I burst into tears because I knew that was not my mama. That was me. Then he said, "I see you kneeling over by the side of your house crying out to God to help you with this." I really was squalling then because I saw in my mind one night in particular that I knelt by a wall inside a room and cried so hard for God to help me. "Don't worry anymore because God is going to deliver you tonight," he said. He prayed a prayer of deliverance and I went back to my seat.

The next day I wasn't jealous anymore. My daughter, Debbie, asked me what the preacher said to me when he put the microphone down. I wouldn't tell her because I was ashamed that I had let the devil put jealousy on me.

I was fine for a year or two. One day Debbie and I were talking and she asked me again what E. L. Terry had said to me. I thought it would be okay to tell her so I did. Evidently by discussing it, I cracked open a door that let the devil put it on me again.

Jealousy was back only this time it was worse. It was eating me up. I fussed at the least little thing, made my husband's life miserable, and hindered his ministry. I didn't know how to be free again so I decided that I would take control and not say anything that even hinted that I was jealous.

Finally we moved from that church and I made up my mind that I would not be jealous of anyone at the next. That didn't last long. I became jealous again, but was determined that nobody would know. I kept my mouth shut and tried my best to hide it, but occasionally mean things about that woman came out of my mouth. *Out of the abundance of the heart the mouth speaks.*

I began attending a prayer meeting at Janie Tarpley's house on Tuesday mornings. They were so exciting I could hardly wait to get there.

Just before I woke up one Tuesday morning, I had a dream. In the dream I was preparing for a new job, one that I had never done before. I would be a waitress.

My husband was driving me to the job when I looked down and saw two big spots on my garment. I thought, *I can't go to work like this with these spots on my uniform.* Then I remembered that I would wear an apron which would cover the spots and no one would know they were there. I found my apron, put it on and sure enough it hid the spots, but when I looked down I could see beneath the apron and knew they were still there. I decided they would dry and hardly leave a stain. Nobody would know.

As we neared the restaurant I looked down again and saw that I was barefooted. You see, I wasn't wearing the shoes of peace the Bible speaks of putting on which helps you walk in peace with others. Jealousy and peace do not travel together on the same path.

There was more to the dream which I will cover in a later chapter. When I awoke I asked God, "What were the two spots?"

I heard in my spirit, *jealousy and resentment.*

When I arrived at the prayer meeting, I told my dream and asked for prayer. The women prayed and I was delivered. I didn't feel anything, but trusted in my heart that it was taken care of. It was. I have been free since.

Janie warned me against letting jealousy and resentment return. She said to rebuke any feelings of it that came. It was wonderful to finally be free. It made such a difference in our ministry. Yes, there was always someone I could have been jealous of, but I rebuked the thought and thanked God for his help.

SPIRIT OF INFERIORITY

For many years if I was in the company of a highly educated person, I could hardly carry on a conversation because of a spirit of inferiority. Though I played the piano for years, if someone was at church who knew how to play I hit many wrong notes.

I had always admired the wonderful sounds Vesta Kerce made on the piano at state camp meetings. Finally I was privileged to take lessons from her. I felt so inferior in her presence I could hardly play my songs that I had practiced all week.

She told me that there will always be someone who plays the piano better than both of us. I argued that nobody could play better than her.

She said, "Plenty of people play better, but that does not excuse me from doing the best I can do with what God has given me."

I realize now there will always be someone who is more talented, prettier, richer, or smarter than you or me. We have to accept that fact and go on with what God called us to do with the abilities we have and not feel inferior to those who we think excel us.

Through Lesa Henderson's prayer at our Set Free meetings at Alton I am free of that spirit of inferiority.

FORGIVE

Our salvation, deliverance and healing hinges on our forgiveness of others.

Jesus said, *For if ye forgive men their trespasses, your heavenly Father will also forgive you. But if ye forgive not men their trespasses, neither will your Father forgive your trespasses (Matthew 6:14-15).*

Then came Peter to him, and said, Lord, how oft shall my brother sin against me, and I forgive him? Till seven times? Jesus saith unto him, I say not unto thee, until seven times: but, until seventy times seven (Mtthew 18:21-22).

And his lord was wroth, and delivered him to the tormentors, till he should pay all that was due unto him. So likewise shall my heavenly Father do also unto you, if ye from your hearts forgive not everyone his brother their trespasses (Matthew 18:34-35).

Forgive and ye shall be forgiven (Luke 6:37).

To whom ye forgive anything, I forgive also: for if I forgave anything, to whom I forgave it, for your sakes forgave I it in the person of Christ; Lest Satan should get an advantage of us: for we are not ignorant of his devices (II Corinthians 2:10-11).

Don't let Satan take advantage of you through un-forgiveness. It is one of his devices. If you have trouble in this area, tell God that you are willing to forgive. Ask Him to help you and to forgive through you. Believe He is doing it.

Be healed of your hurts and be set free of demonic oppression.

GOD CAN DELIVER YOU FROM ANY EVIL SPIRIT

When I was a child, I learned that God still delivered from demons. We were visiting family in Tampa. One evening, Mama, Daddy, my two sisters and I piled into the car. Mama said we were going to pray for a cousin.

"What's wrong with her?" I asked.

"She wants to be saved," Mama answered. "She needs deliverance."

"What does that mean?"

"It means she's an alcoholic and it may be caused by demons. If so, we'll have to cast them out."

It got real quiet as we traveled down the road. After a while mama said, "Girls, stay in the car while your Daddy and I go in. Be real quiet and reverent and pray. Demons look for another body to inhabit when they have to leave the one they're in."

The three of us nodded with our eyes big and round. It was just beginning to get dark when we arrived at the house. We sisters huddled together in the back seat and whispered as Mama and Daddy went in to pray. We hoped they would be back soon.

We were parked on the edge of a field. Daddy parked away from the house, so we girls would not hear whatever would happen. It had gotten dark, but the moon allowed us to see outlines of the houses and bushes nearby.

Then we heard it. A noise left the house with a big commotion and headed our way moaning as it came. We looked to see what made the noise, but could see nothing.

Whatever it was went into the bushes shaking them and groaning loudly. It sounded like an angry person was pitching a temper tantrum. The short stubby bushes moved and the empty field shone in the moonlight. Nobody was there. Then the noise went to the next bush and shook it and continued until it faded in the distance.

We decided it must be the demons trying to find somebody to enter. We really prayed then and did what Mama always did - we pled the blood of Jesus.

If you are tormented by anything, plead the blood of Jesus over yourself and command all evil spirits to leave you. If you don't get deliverance, ask another believer to help you pray. God wants you free.

PART III

ARMOR IS FOR YOUR PROTECTION!

It does nothing to the enemy!

EPHESIANS 6: 10 - 18

Wherefore take unto you the whole armor of God, that ye may be able to withstand in the evil day, and having done all - to stand. (a military phrase – Having conquered all, stand, ready to do battle again)

Stand therefore, having your loins girt about with truth, and having on the breastplate of righteousness;

And your feet shod with the preparation of the gospel of peace;

Above all, taking the shield of faith, wherewith ye shall be able to quench all the fiery darts of the wicked.

And take the helmet of salvation, and the sword of the Spirit, which is the word of God:

Praying always with all prayer and supplication in the Spirit, watching thereunto with all perseverance and supplication for all saints . . .

INVADING TERMITES

Tala the termite, his wife, children, and in-laws lived in our house before we bought it for retirement. We saw a few telltale signs on the surface of the walls, but not until our son, Mike, tore the sheet-rock off to expose the inside did we see the true damage. Tala, with family and friends had eaten into beams that held up the middle of the house. Many boards had to be replaced. Had the bugs been left to eat away at the house, it eventually would have been a cement block hull with all the inside gone - eaten away by termites.

The termite is a very small critter, yet he has great destructive potential. Tala, along with his wife Tassie, his son Trundel, his daughter Tiny, and other family members and friends can destroy a building millions of times bigger than they and do it in record time. Tala Termite I nc. came in through a crack in the foundation. They invaded at night while the homeowner slept, sneaky little things. The owner was unaware of their presence until Tala and the whole gang showed themselves by swarming out in the open after the damage was done.

We have an enemy who loves to invade our spiritual house when we least expect it. He hides to do his dirty work. When he has destroyed a life he reveals himself. We see too late it was the enemy of our soul - Satan and his demons. Before destruction comes, let's be warned of the signs of the terrible invading termites. Once we are aware of their presence we can call on the mighty exterminator, Jesus, to help us get rid of the pesky little creatures. He will use the Holy Ghost spray to eliminate them before they eliminate us.

Since Satan and his cohorts cannot touch the SPIRIT of the Christian, this section will help you examine every conceivable spot in your SOUL and BODY, the parts of you he can oppress. Your soul is your mind, will, and emotions.

Here we go on a spiritual termite inspection! Let's see if we can get Tala and the gang before they get us!

FIRST ARTICLE OF ARMOR

GIRDLE OF TRUTH

Having your loins girt about with truth.

We women often wear a girdle! It helps us hold in our stomach. We do it to make us look better, but there is another benefit - it assists our back, especially if it is weak. The first piece of armor to put on for protection in this war against invading termites is the girdle of truth.

My mother-in-law gave birth to eight strong, healthy, and beautiful babies. I have often thought what a strong woman she was to carry and give birth to so many children. I heard her say many times as she dressed for the day, "I have to put on this girdle. It holds my back in place. After having eight young' uns I need all the help I can get." That girdle protected and comforted her back so that she could work in a women's fashion store until she was seventy-six-years old.

As Christians who want to give birth or help the babies we have already seen born into the kingdom of God, we, like my mother in law, 'need all the help we can get.' So, let's put on the girdle of truth.

THE GIRDLE OF TRUTH PROTECTS OUR LOINS

The Hebrew word for loins is *chalats* which means the seat of vigor or strength. It is the area of our body between the waist and hip that houses the reproductive organs. These organs in men and women carry the sperm and seed that bring about the re-creation of a new life. In this area of a woman's body is located the womb - the section of a woman that carries and nurtures a baby.

GIVING BIRTH

As a Christian, we have two major responsibilities. The first one is to *birth* others into the kingdom of God and the second is to *teach* them the ways of God. *

First the birthing. We bring others into the kingdom by *witness* and *prayer*. When we *witness* we have bad news and good news. "The bad news," we tell them, "is that all have sinned and come short of the glory of God. We all need a Savior. The first man and woman, Adam and Eve, sinned in the Garden of Eden. The sin separated them from God who is holy and cannot fellowship with sin; therefore He no longer walked with them in the cool of the day. A lack of His presence left an empty spot in them. The hollow feeling was passed down to all mankind. We all have it. We all feel lonely and long to know God as Adam did in the beginning."

When a person understands their need for God we tell them the good news: *Jesus died to cleanse you from your sins and bring you back to God.* He paid the penalty for sin that Adam brought on us all. By accepting Jesus' death on the cross, we are restored back to fellowship with God. Now we can talk to Him again and know that He hears us. The empty hole that only God can fill overflows with His presence.

TEACHING THE TRUTH

Now we must *teach* them the truth. If we do not *know* the truth we cannot *teach* it to our babies.

Jesus said of the Scribes and Pharisees, *Woe unto to you, scribes (teachers of the law) and Pharisees, hypocrites! You compass sea and land to make one proselyte, (win a single convert) and when he is made, you make him two fold more the child of hell than yourselves (Matthew 23:15).*

The Scribes and Pharisees to whom Jesus spoke did not know the truth; therefore they reproduced converts who were in greater error than they. We do not want to do that. We desire to reproduce true believers. We do not want to be a bad example because a person brought into the kingdom of God tends to be like the one who led them to Christ. The girdle of truth assures that we know the truth; therefore we can teach it to those we win.

REPRODUCE KINGS

God said to Jacob in Genesis 35:11, *Kings shall come out of thy loins.* It is God's desire that we reproduce spiritual kings and queens for His kingdom. Do you want it said of you, "Kings have come from her?" I do.

God is the spiritual sperm that impregnates the seed of the spirit for the new birth. The Holy Spirit is the womb that carries it. The blood of Jesus gives it life. Prayer is the push that brings it forth. The Bible or Word of God is the water that cleanses it with that first bath. The baby's food is the milk of the Word of God. We hold the bottle to the

79

infant's mouth when we instruct the new born in the truth. Our own eyes must first be opened to the truth to lead others into it for Jesus said, *If the blind lead the blind they will both fall in the ditch (Mt. 15:14).*

A newborn is covered with streaks of blood and a thick, white substance known as vernix caseosa. The infant must be bathed immediately.

I watched as the nurse washed my first grandbaby, Justin. There I stood at the window looking in. The nurse lay Justin on her left arm with his small head cradled in the palm of her hand. She walked to a large sink. With her right hand rubbed soap on his little body and head. He had lots of dark hair. She rinsed his head by holding the top of it under the running water. I can still see the picture in my mind. She was an expert at getting just enough of his head under the water to rinse it.

God is more skillful than that when He cleanses us from the pollution of sin. He holds us in His big hand and lathers us with the soap of His Word and submerges us under the fountain of the blood of Jesus where we are cleansed in our spirit. Then as we grow we read the Word and are taught by Godly people until we have our mind changed and renewed.

A DREAM

Once I dreamed of a new born baby who was wrapped in gauze. The baby could not move because of the constriction of the bandage. A terrible odor oozed from under the gauze. I thought, *somebody needs to unwrap this baby and give him a bath.* No one else was around so I began to un-wind the gauze. To my surprise, the odor left on its own as I un-wrapped him and I did not have to bathe him. Immediately, the baby matured and sat up alone. I took him by the hand and he walked. I was amazed that the baby could walk so soon after birth.

God let me know through my dream that when a baby is born into the kingdom of God we must pray until they are free of all the bondages of sin. Prayer unwraps them. When they get free, God will take away the stink of sin. We don't have to wash them or clean them up. He does that. He also matures them and they soon walk spiritually. We hold their hand by teaching them the truth.

A VISION

My friend, Janie Tarpley, saw in the spirit, the altar in a church. She watched as little babies were born, but at the end of the altar sat a ferocious lion. He snatched up many of the new born infants and ate them. The Bible says, *The devil as a roaring lion, walketh about seeking whom he may devour (I Peter 5:8). He came to kill, steal and destroy (John 10:10).* He is waiting at the altar of salvation to devour the tender life of a new born Christian.

It is our responsibility after praying them into the kingdom to protect them from the devouring lion by teaching them the truth. The Bible says that knowing the truth will set us free - free from the devouring lion, Satan.

LUST OF THE FLESH

Not only is the LOINS the place of reproduction but it is also the seat of lust. This is the spot where lust breeds and is fulfilled. Lust is our number one enemy. It is more powerful than drugs or alcohol. Lust attacks every living person in one form or another, some time in their life. Lust wars in our body. It wars against our spirit man.

The Bible speaks of two types of lust. One is the lust of the flesh and two is the lust of the eyes. Let's look at the lust of the flesh.

FOOD

Lust for food is the most common of all lusts of the flesh. It is an appetite out of control. The Bible also calls it gluttony. This lust is accompanied with *dissatisfaction and a complaining spirit.* In Psalms 78 we see the *dissatisfaction* of the people of God. Though God did wonderful miracles for them in the wilderness, they were not grateful, but *complained.*

He brought them out of slavery in Egypt, where they were abused and forced to work vigorously. Still they wanted to return to Egypt because of the garlic and onions there. Their taste buds tugged at them to go back to slavery.

They complained against Moses and Aaron and said that they wished they had died in Egypt when they sat by the flesh pots and ate bread until they were full. They accused Moses of leading them into the wilderness to die of hunger.

It was a complaint against God since He is the one who told Moses to lead them out of bondage. God who created them knew their need for food. He created them to need a certain amount to live.

God is gracious. In His mercy He rained down food from the sky. The food was called manna. It came straight from heaven every day except Saturday. There was always enough for every person. On Friday they gathered sufficiently for Saturday, their Sabbath, and it did not spoil. If they were gluttonous and collected double on other days it rotted and stunk. Worms grew in it and they could not eat it.

In spite of God's provision of the food they needed, still they were not happy. They wanted meat to eat. *They tempted God in their heart by asking meat for their lust (Psalm 78:18).*

The Hebrew word for lust in this Scripture is *nephesh*. It means a breathing creature, (ie) animal or vitality, any appetite, beast, body, desire, greedy, lust, man, me, mind, one, own, person, pleasure, (x) would have it.

It sounds to me like lust means a breathing person who greedily craves with animal desires or appetites to bring pleasure to one's own self. It begins in the mind but if entertained causes the person to do anything to have it.

God gave the children of Israel the thing they lusted for, but He was angry about it. He said that He had already given them angel's food to eat. Since they were un-happy with that, *He rained flesh also upon them as dust, and feathered fowls like as the sand of the sea. And he let it fall in the midst of their camp, round about their habitations. So they did eat and were well filled: for he gave them their own desire (lust) (Psalms 78:27-29).*

LARGEST QUAIL HUNT IN HISTORY

Numbers 11:31-32 and Psalm 78:27--29 tells us about the largest quail hunt in history. Many quails are said to visit Egypt during the spring months, crossing the Red Sea into the Sinai Peninsula. One writer tells of them coming into Italy in great numbers, and so exhausted with long flight that if they sighted a boat so many would settle thereon that it would sink it. Quails multiply in such numbers as to form clouds in migration. Mother-birds lay from 12 to 20 eggs each, in a season.

Quails always fly with the wind when crossing a body of water lest they tire so much they fall. In the case of Israel's feast of quails, God simply caused them to fly out of their regular course by a strong wind, and thus made them come near the camp of Israel a day's journey all around. They came flying 2 cubits (slightly over 4 feet counting 25 inches to the cubit) above the ground so they could be conveniently caught and killed - some to be dried in the sun for future use.

The people killed quails for two full days and one night. Each of the men killed about 105 bushels apiece. Since the Bible says the people gathered quails, implying all grownups and not the men of war only, let us suppose that at least three million of the more than six million people estimated took part in this quail hunt. On the basis of a dressed quail being the size of a pint container, with 64 pints to the bushel we can figure that the one who gathered the least (105 Bushels) had 6,720 pints, or 6,720 quails in his heap. All of the 3 million grownups gathering no more than the least amount would bring the total to 20,160,000,000 quails. Counting these to be worth the low estimate of $1.00 each on today's market, we see that the greedy Israelites most likely gathered upwards of 20 billion dollars worth of quails! *

*Dake

The Bible says, *They were not estranged from their lust; but while their meat was yet in their mouths, The wrath of God came upon them, and slew the fattest of them, and smote down the chosen men of Israel (Psalms 78:27-31).*

Another scripture says: *while the meat was still between their teeth, before they had finished chewing, the wrath of the Lord was kindled against the people, and the Lord smote the people with a very great plague* (Numbers 11:33).

Their lust for meat killed them! *He named the place Kib'roth-hat-ta'a-vah because there they buried the people that lusted (Numbers 11:34).* The word Kib'roth-hat-ta'a-vah means *graves of the longing.* Their longing for food took them to the grave.

God is saying that the people desired meat for their pleasure. It was in their mind. They did not need it for their health. They were very healthy on the manna God provided. Not one of them was sick or feeble. In spite of that they were not satisfied, but desired more. They wanted meat to eat. This was a form of lust.

What about our appetite? Do we want to eat more than we need for our health's sake? Overeating is the cause of many diseases.

Eating an improper diet is another cause for disease. Once I had an infection that I could not get cured. I went to the doctor several times and took the medicine he prescribed. The infection lingered. Finally in desperation I sought another doctor. He prescribed the same type of medication I had already taken. I complained to him that I had taken that medication and after weeks of treatment, I still had the infection.

His next words shocked me. He said, "Don't eat anything with sugar in it and you'll get well."

I was disappointed. I didn't want to give up sugar. I loved sugar. I lusted for sugar. After thinking about it, I did cut back on my desserts and guess what? I got well.

Another time I gave up sugar completely. This time I ate a diet of food and supplements programmed just for me and perfectly balanced for the proper PH. I got well of every ailment I had. Even adhesions from surgery disappeared. When I stopped eating the proper food and started back eating sugar gradually new diseases appeared. I developed high blood pressure and had a mild heart attack. Bronchitis returned, and other ailments. I am convinced that God's formula for diet in the Bible is for my benefit. It isn't easy to follow but it works.

Not long ago, the doctors told my husband to lose weight and he could come off of all his medications. When God spoke against us fulfilling the lusts of the flesh, He meant it for the good of our health.

The girdle of truth will help me to rid myself of lust for food and fight off diseases in the natural body. For those diseases that cannot be controlled by diet, the girdle of truth tells me that Jesus took my sicknesses to the cross. With His stripes I am healed.

SEX

The second most predominant lust of the flesh is sex. Sex between two married people is not a sin nor is it lust; however, it can convert into lust. God initiated it for the procreation of the human race. It is a beautiful expression of love between a man and his wife. God laid down laws to govern sex and to keep it pure. First of all He said, let every man have his own wife. He said, *let the man leave his father and mother and cleave to his wife. The two will become one flesh.* This describes the sex act.

He said, *rejoice with the wife of your youth. Let her be as the loving hind and pleasant roe; let her breasts satisfy thee at all times; and be thou ravished always with her love (Proverbs 5:18-19).* He said in I Corinthians 7:3, *Render due benevolence to each other.* In other words, meet each other's needs sexually. He did not say to meet each other's lusts, but to *keep the bed pure.* (Hebrews 13:4 NIV)

Sex between two people who are married, but not to each other is a sin. It is called adultery. Jesus warned in His

Sermon on the Mount about the danger of adultery. One of the Ten Commandments is *do not commit adultery.* Jesus said do not even lust after a woman (Matthew 5:28). You are guilty already of committing adultery in your heart if you do.

God did not make these rules to be mean to us and deny us of a good time. He did it to give us a wonderful life, free from heartache and disease. He wants your spiritual house to stand. He does not want the termites of lust to invade and begin destroying the foundation of your house.

Paul warned us against the dangers of adultery and fornication when he said, *Flee fornication. Every sin that a man does is without the body; but he that committeth fornication sins against his own body. What ? Know ye not that your body is the temple of the Holy Ghost . . . Therefore honor God in your body (I Corinthians 6:18-20).*

When you stay pure sexually, you prevent many diseases from attacking your body, and you also honor God. That is a win/win situation: pleasing God and protecting yourself. Satan tries to pollute every beautiful thing that God has made. Lust is Satan's substitute for love. Don't be trapped into believing Satan's lies and falling into the trap of lust. Know the truth of God's Word and be free.

I remember my father teaching that every woman has the same body parts and equipment. If a married man understood that his own wife has everything that he needs he would not run around looking for a new partner. That sounds very simplistic yet it is true. Study married couples who have committed adultery and those who have divorced. Generally they are not happier with the second mate. I know there are always exceptions. But usually they were happier with the first mate. Try to work out your problems and be happy, as the Bible says, *with the wife of your youth.* You will save your children a lot of heartache and pain as well as your mate and yourself.

If you are a wife, remember that you have the tools to make your own husband happy. Use what God has given you. Help prevent lust in you both. Read Marrabell Morgan's book - Total Woman - or - You Can Be The Wife of a Happy Husband - by Darien B. Cooper.

Husbands, love and cherish your wife as Christ loved the church and gave Himself for it. You both will be happier. Men read the book - Do Yourself a Favor Love Your Wife, and - Man of Steel and Velvet.

Husbands and wives, treat your marriage partner right and you won't have to find a new one. Each one comes with a different set of problems. The next one could be worse. You could be jumping out of the frying pan into the fire.

ORAL SEX

Recently I read a shocking article in a magazine in a doctor's office. The article stated alarming statistics concerning children and oral sex - a large number of 4th graders, 9 year olds, are having oral sex at school. The article went on to say that 65 percent of middle school children, ages 10 to 12, are engaging in oral sex at school. That it is considered the "cool thing to do." The "in crowd" participates. Sick and saddened, I continued to read that an alarming number of these children are getting diseases in their mouth and throat. It was almost more than I could bear to read. I remembered that the sins of the parents are multiplied in the children. This sin is very common among adults. You may say, "Is it sin with your marriage partner?" In my opinion it is un-natural. God did not intend sex in this manner. It is one of the lusts of the flesh and is considered unclean. Pray and ask God.

MASTURBATION

This subject is not one we want to talk about. It is a very private matter. I am embarrassed to mention it, but I believe it is another form of lust, one that we can have victory over. I remember as a child knowing that self gratification was wrong. No one had to tell me. I knew it instinctively. After accepting Jesus at a young age, I overcame this form of lust; therefore I know that you can overcome. If left open, it allows other sins to enter. Let's close this door through the power of Jesus. You can be delivered. Commit your dreams to the Lord.

PORNOGRAPHY

There is suddenly a big increase in pornography. We hear about it on Christian television and news programs. Many good people, adults and children, are hooked to it through the internet. I hear of young children, who while trying to look up information on the computer for a school report, have tapped into pornography.

Once a person sees an ungodly picture it is stuck in his mind. It is nearly impossible to erase. Satan loves to replay the pictures over and over. Lust enters and sets up camp. The person is drawn back again and again.

Pray for your pastors as many ministers are falling prey to this trap. It starts innocently, unintentionally. But it ends many times with the minister becoming so entrapped that he acts upon the scenes he watches. Soon another soldier is down wallowing in the gutter of sin. His life in shambles with his testimony gone, the respect of his children lost, his marriage ruined and his credibility with his church demolished. Is there restitution?

Yes. It comes through the truth. You must know the truth for the truth to set you free.

Am I saying that the internet is wrong? No. But I am saying that we need to use every precaution to stay away from pornography on it. Don't fall for it. Don't let Satan have that hold on you.

HOMOSEXUALITY

Many people who live the homosexual lifestyle say that they are born that way. They say that God made them to be gay or lesbian. That is not the truth but one of Satan's lies. Homosexuality is a form of lust.

In one of the Scriptures that mentions homosexual activity, the Greek word for lust is *orexis*. It means *excitement of the mind* (ie.) *longing after*. It comes from another Greek word *oregonai* that means *to reach out after*. You see you were not born that way. You became *excited in your mind*. You *longed after* the wrong thing. You had to leave your natural sexual tendencies and *reach out after* that life style. Homosexuality is against nature. It is not the natural form of sex, the form that God intended.

The cause of homosexuality according to the Bible is *not honoring God and being unthankful.*

God created us male and female for a purpose, reproduction. We dishonor God's plan for us when we disregard the way He made us. We are not thankful for who we are and His sexual plan for us. That leads to a wicked imagination and we are blinded to the truth. In this state of mind, one commits the perverse act of uncleanness. We thumped our nose at Him and changed His plan for our sexual life into perversion.

Here is the way the Bible says it.

> *But God shows his anger from heaven against all sinful evil men who push away the truth from them. For the truth about God is known to them instinctively; God has put this knowledge in their hearts. Since earliest times men have seen the earth and sky and all God made, and have known of his existence and great eternal power. So they will have no excuse (when they stand before God at Judgment Day). Yes, they knew about him all right, but they wouldn't admit it or worship him or even thank him for all his daily care. And after awhile they began to think up silly ideas of what God was like and what he wanted them to do. The result was that their foolish minds became dark and confused. Claiming themselves to be wise without God they became utter fools instead . . . So God let them go*

ahead into every sort of sex sin, and do whatever they wanted to - yes, vile and sinful things with each other's bodies. Instead of believing what they knew was the truth about God, they deliberately chose to believe lies. So they prayed to the things God made, but wouldn't obey the blessed God who made these things.

That is why God let go of them and let them do all these evil things, so that even their women turned against God's natural plan for them and indulged in sex sin with each other. And the men instead of having a normal sex relationship with women, burned with lust for each other, men doing shameful things with other men and, as a result, getting paid within their own souls with the penalty they so richly deserved (Romans1:18-27 LB).

Thou shalt not lie with mankind, as with woman kind: it is abomination (Lev. 18:22).

The word abomination in Hebrew is *toebah* and means something disgusting, abhorrence especially idolatry.

Webster's Dictionary says that abominable means: away from man, inhuman, nasty, disgusting, vile, loathsome, highly unpleasant, disagreeable, very bad, anything hateful and disgusting.

"Know ye not that the unrighteous shall not inherit the kingdom of God Be not deceived: neither fornicators, nor idolaters, nor adulterers, nor effeminate, nor abusers of themselves with mankind, nor thieves, nor covetous, nor

drunkards, nor revilers, nor extortioners, shall inherit the kingdom of God" (I Corinthians 6:9-10).

There is no doubt from these Scriptures that the homosexual life style is not God's plan for your life. God has a much better plan. The next verse in the above Scripture says, *And such were some of you but you are washed, but you are sanctified, but you are justified in the name of the Lord Jesus, and by the Spirit of our God.*

That can be you! You can be cleansed. Would you like to be free of that life style? The Bible says, y*ou shall know the truth and the truth will set you free. (John 8:32)* Read and accept the Word of God, know the truth, and yes you will be free.

WHAT IS THE GIRDLE OF TRUTH?

You may be wondering where is my help for being free of these lusts of the flesh? Let me tell you that there is hope and help. The girdle of truth is God's answer for you. You are wondering where do I get it and how do I put it on. Hang on. I'm about to tell you.

WHAT IS TRUTH?

I hear the question echo through Pilate's Judgment Hall. Jesus told Pilate that He, Jesus, came into this world to bear witness of the truth and that everyone that is of the truth hears His voice. Then Pilate asked the question that we have asked many times, "What is truth?"

Let's look at the Bible for our answer. John said, *The law was given by Moses but grace and truth came by*

Jesus Christ (John 1:17). That's our first clue. Truth was brought to us by Jesus.

JESUS IS THE TRUTH

Jesus was born to a virgin, which means that Mary had never known a man sexually. The Holy Spirit of God came over her and she became pregnant with Jesus. He was born sinless to be a sacrifice for our sins. His cousin John saw Him one day as He walked along the sea shore. He pointed to Jesus and said, *"Behold the Lamb of God who taketh away the sins of the world."*

When Jesus was 33 years old, John's statement was fulfilled. Crucified on a cross, Jesus became our sacrifice for sin. He took with Him to the cross everything you or I have ever done wrong. He bore the sins of every person in the whole world and all who will ever be born.

If we ask, He will forgive us and help us to overcome those sins That is the truth. Jesus, himself, said *I am the way, the truth and the life (John 1:6).* JESUS IS TRUTH.

I was eight years old when I accepted Jesus as the truth. I felt as if I were a terrible sinner even though I was too young to have done a lot of wrong things. But I knew that I was born in sin. The Bible told me that we all were born in sin. Feeling the guilt of sin confirmed what I was taught. I was miserable.

Kneeling at the altar in church, I confessed my sins because the Bible says that if we confess our sins He is faithful and just to forgive us our sins and to cleanse us from all unrighteousness. What a load was lifted that night! I was not afraid that I was going to go to hell anymore. I had wonderful peace of mind. I was born again. I knew Jesus said that unless you are born of water and the spirit you cannot enter into the kingdom of heaven. Now I was born of the spirit. We call it the new birth or being saved. I was saved! That was the TRUTH. I knew in my own heart that Jesus is the TRUTH.

THE HOLY SPIRIT IS THE TRUTH

My father preached and I read in the Bible that Jesus said, *"I will pray the Father and he will give you another comforter that he may abide with you forever; Even the SPIRIT OF TRUTH; Whom the world cannot receive, because it seeth him not neither knoweth him; but ye know him: for he dwelleth with you, and shall be in you (John 14:16-17).*

The comforter, which is the Holy Ghost, whom the Father will send in my name, he shall teach you all things, and bring all things to your remembrance, whatsoever I have said unto you (John 14:26).

Nevertheless I tell you the truth; It is expedient for you that I go away; for if I go not away, The comforter will not come unto you; but if I depart, I will send him unto you (John 16:7).

Howbeit when he, the SPIRIT OF TRUTH is come, he will guide you into all TRUTH . . . and he will shew you things to come. 14 He shall glorify me: for he shall receive of mine, and shall shew it unto you" (John 16:13).

I wanted the comforter, the very Spirit of truth, to come inside me. He promised to show me the truth and to guide me into all truth. He would show me things to come and show me things about Jesus and God the Father. I was eager to know more. I began to pray for this experience of receiving the gift of the Holy Spirit. I expected it to be like my father's experience.

DADDY'S EXPERIENCE

My father, Yates Warren Kidd, was a minister who preached many sermons. My favorite was when he told of his experience of receiving the gift of the Holy Spirit, THE SPIRIT OF TRUTH.

My father met God on the highway in his truck as he delivered feed. That day he threw away his bottle of whiskey that he always carried in the seat of his truck right next to him. He was delivered of alcohol in a moment of time: however he did not totally surrender his life to God.

That same day my mother realized that she needed to go to church and find God. She had an encounter with God in her bed that night and was born again by praying a two word prayer. She simply cried out, "Oh, God!" She and Daddy went to church the following Sunday.

Daddy was not ready to 'sell out' to Jesus yet. When he was a young boy he had an experience with God, but had wandered far away from Him and the truth. He went to several services and heard the Bible taught. Finally the night came when he knew it was decision time. He felt that he must know where he stood with God. He knelt at the altar that night determined to know his standing with God.

Very timidly he tried to pray but he didn't know what to say. Having much pride he felt that everyone was looking at him. He could visualize that all of his friends had come into the church after he knelt and were staring at him and laughing. With his head down, he struggled to know what to do.

He opened his eyes with his head still down and saw the pastor of the church pass in front of him. Reaching out he grabbed the pants leg of the pastor, Jake Roberts. Brother Roberts leaned over to see what he wanted. Softly, Daddy said, "Brother Roberts, pray for me."

Brother Roberts patted him on the head and said, "God, bless this boy." That was all of his prayer. He walked on.

Satan began to talk to Daddy. "Nobody wants to pray for you. Everybody wants to go home. See, even the preacher doesn't care anything for you. He's tired and wants to leave. Why don't you get up from here so everybody can go home. You are making a fool of yourself."

Daddy said he turned around and said to the people sitting in the church waiting for him to finish praying. "If any of you want to go home it's okay. You can go ahead. Don't wait for me. I am going to be here until I hear from heaven or time to go to work in the morning, - whichever comes first. I have to know where I stand with God, tonight!" He turned back around and started to pray again. This time it was easier and several people came up and began to pray with him. In a few minutes he was praying fervently.

Suddenly, he fell back in the floor. As he lay there a shaft of light began to open from heaven. It got wider until it was as wide as his body. The light had the most beautiful colors that streamed down on him coming right out of heaven. An object floated down the shaft of light. As it got closer to him he saw that it was in the form of a dove. When the dove reached him and landed on his chest it felt as if a man's hand had slapped him on the chest. The dove quivered and went inside. His tongue felt thick and he began to speak in a different language.

He had received the baptism of the Holy Ghost as recorded in the second chapter of the book of Acts. Daddy knew that night where he stood with God. He knew that he was right with God. He had received the SPIRIT OF TRUTH!

When he got up from the altar, Daddy knew immediately that he was called to preach the Gospel. He said that he felt the weight of a lost world fall on his shoulders. He preached the truth as the Spirit guided him into the ministry. The Spirit of Truth led him for the rest of his life. He lived one of the most TRUTHFUL lives of anyone I know. (Read more of his story in my book – Kidd and Spitfire Doll)

MY EXPERIENCE

Having heard this story several times, I longed to have the same experience. I imagined that the same dove would descend on me and I would see the ray of light. But it didn't happen that way. I went to the altar almost every night that we had church to ask God to give me the gift of the Holy Spirit. I knew that it was real and I knew that God wanted me to have it. Daddy had taught that and I had read it in the Bible. I knew that what the Bible said about it was true but I couldn't seem to receive the experience. I prayed and cried for long periods of time after most services.

Finally, after months of praying, the night came when I knew that I would receive the blessing of the Holy Ghost. When the altar call was given, I marched to the front expecting to receive the gift. I knelt, raised my hands and began to praise God. I was immediately lost in the Spirit and spoke in tongues as the Spirit gave the utterance. I hardly knew what was happening. I didn't cry or beg or fall back in the floor. I didn't see a vision or have a dove land on me but I received the promise of the Father in heaven.

I knew He said, *"You shall receive the gift of the Holy Ghost. For the promise is unto you and to your children and to all that are afar off, even as many as the Lord our God shall call"* *(Acts 2:38-39)*. I knew that I was one of those who were afar off and called of the Lord.

When I arose from the altar and sat, the Holy Spirit got in my feet and came up my legs. Before I realized what was happening, I was on my feet dancing in the Spirit from one side of the church to the other, with my hands raised toward heaven.

A man who was at the other end of the altar received the Spirit the same time that I did. He too was walking back and forth, praising God with his hands in the air. He was eighty-two-years-old I was nine. Both the young and the old, male and female, received the Spirit of Truth that night.

God said, *"I will pour out my spirit on all flesh. Your sons and your daughters shall prophesy and your young men shall see visions, and your old men shall dream dreams. On my servants and on my handmaidens I will pour out in those days of my Spirit; and they shall prophesy" (Acts 2:17-18).*

I was different after that. Condemnation, guilt and fear had to leave. Gradually, I stopped apologizing to my family for things I had not done. I stopped worrying about imaginary sins - sins I had not even thought about much less committed. I stopped being afraid of slipping and doing something wrong.

I had the comforter and the helper - the one who lives in me to guide me into all truth. He was on the job leading me in the right direction. He has comforted and helped me more times than I can remember in the sixty plus years since then. I would not give him up for anything in the world.

(For the rest of the story read Kidd's Daughter Another Spitfire.)

MY HUSBAND'S EXPERIENCE

Malcolm, my husband, had a totally different experience than my father or I. A group of his teenage friends met after school several days in a row. They went down to Lake Waccamaw close to his home town of

Whiteville, North Carolina to race their cars around the lake. One day his friend looked for him but could not find him. They were going to the lake again. They left to race without Malcolm. A young man died that day as his car plunged into a watery grave.

God had a different plan for Malcolm's life. After he attended his best friend's funeral, conviction seized him. He went out that night and tried to party and forget the accident. But he kept thinking, *I was supposed to be in that car. I had been in it every other day that week.*

He knew his mother prayed for him and that old Sister Powers prayed for him daily too. She reminded him each time he attended church by saying, "Malcolm, I am praying for you. God has his hand on your life. You are going to be a preacher!"

That night about midnight he went home and knocked on the door. His parents always locked the door when he was out at night so they knew what time he came in. They didn't come to the door immediately and he worried that the Lord had come and left him. Ministers talked about the rapture a lot back then.

When they opened the door, he said, "Take me to the preacher's house. I've got to have help." They went to the church where the pastor and his wife lived and knocked on the doors to the Sunday school rooms - the pastor's living quarters. Sleepily the pastor opened the door and invited them in.

Malcolm told him that he wanted to get saved. He immediately dropped to his knees and they began to pray.

The next thing Malcolm knew he was getting up out from under the kitchen table where he had rolled while praying. He didn't remember how it happened. He just knew that he crawled out from under the table speaking in another language, one that he had not learned, one that was from heaven. He knew that the terrible weight of sin was gone. He was forgiven and cleansed.

His parents led him to the car still speaking in tongues. He spoke for most of the night. He was changed in a flash. He has been different since the moment he put on the GIRDLE of TRUTH. Unlike me, he received Jesus the truth and the Holy Spirit, who is the Spirit of truth, in the same night.

Later when he attended Lee College a man from Nicaragua told him at a men's prayer meeting that when he spoke in tongues he was speaking Spanish in the man's dialect of his home country. He told Malcolm several times what he had said when speaking in tongues. He was always praising God in the man's language, a language that Malcolm had never studied or learned. The spirit of TRUTH knows all languages.

THE WORD OF GOD IS TRUTH

Sanctify them through thy truth; THY WORD IS TRUTH (John 17:17).

Not only is Jesus the truth, and the Holy Spirit is the truth, but the Bible, the Word of God, is the truth. When we read it and listen to God we learn the truth. The Bible cannot be understood completely unless the Spirit of truth reveals the Word to you. He is the revelator. Each time you read the Word, ask Him to uncover the truth. He will. It's His job and He delights in it.

Sanctify comes from the Greek word *hagiazo* and means to make holy, purify or consecrate; (mentally) to venerate. As you read the Word of Truth it will purify you and make you holy if you allow it.

James describes it as a mirror. When we read, we see ourselves with all of our shortcomings. As we read further the Word of God shows us what to do about them. It reveals the truth about each situation in our lives.

Isaiah said in 11:5 *Righteousness will be the girdle of his loins, and faithfulness the girdle of his reins* (Isaiah 11:5).

At the end of this chapter, I will ask you to read a certain portion of the Bible, the Word of Truth. This will help you know the truth. Please take this request seriously and read the assignment.

It can change your life!

HOW DO I PUT ON THE GIRDLE OF TRUTH?

Here are the STEPS one takes to put on the

GIRDLE OF TRUTH.

1. ACCEPT JESUS THE TRUTH

It's as simple as **A,B,C.**

A. Acknowledge that you are a sinner. For all have sinned and come short of the glory of God *(Romans 3:23).*

B. Believe that Jesus is the son of God. That He died and rose from the dead.

That if thou shalt confess with thy mouth the Lord Jesus, and believe in thine heart that God hath raised Him from the dead, thou shalt be saved (Romans 10:9).

C. Confess and repent of your sins.

If we confess our sins, He is faithful and just to forgive us our sins, and to cleanse us from all unrighteousness (I John 1:9).

Pray:

God, I know that I am a sinner. I have done wrong. Please forgive me of all my sins and cleanse me with the blood of Jesus. I believe that Jesus is the son of God. I believe that He died for me and rose again on the third day. I now accept him as my lord and master.

Thank you for saving me and writing my name in the book of life. I desire to know all of the truth of the the Bible. Teach me. Fill me with the Holy Spirit, who will be my comforter, guide, and teacher. I will read the Bible and allow the Holy Spirit to show me what it means. In Jesus name Amen.

_____

(sign your name here)

2. RECEIVE THE SPIRIT OF TRUTH

Continue to believe God for the Holy Spirit Baptism until you know it has happened. You will know because you will speak in tongues and be filled with joy.

The other fruit of the Spirit will begin to manifest in your life also. They are love, joy, peace, longsuffering (patience), gentleness (kindness), goodness, faith (faithfulness), meekness, and temperance (self-control).

3. READ THE WORD OF TRUTH

Read Matthew, Mark, Luke, John and Acts in the Bible three times in a month. To do this you will read 12 chapters a day - six in the morning and six at night. This may sound like a very hard chore to do. Believe me it is not difficult. It will be the joy and strength of your life.

The four writers gave the account of Jesus' ministry in their own words. By reading them three times in a month you will continually read the same stories. You will see Jesus very clearly.

You will understand His ministry and learn what He thought was important. You will hear His heart beat. You will feel His compassion for lost humanity as He forgives sins. You will see His love as He heals the sick. You will watch His desire to see people made whole as He helps the lame man, who hasn't stood in years, stand to His feet and walk! You will feel the power as Jesus raises the dead.

As you learn more about Jesus, you will fall in love with this compassionate, caring person. You will understand that Jesus is the truth through the Word of Truth.

As you read the book of Acts you will see the work of the Holy Spirit. You will see how He carried on the work of Jesus through the apostles after Jesus was gone. How the Holy Spirit is still around and works today in the lives of those who will embrace the Spirit of Truth. As you read you will put on the GIRDLE OF TRUTH!

By putting on the GIRDLE OF TRUTH, you exterminate the termites of lust from your life. Lust cannot live in the presence of the spray of TRUTH.

By putting on the GIRDLE OF TRUTH, you will give birth to babies for the kingdom of God that know the TRUTH for you will teach them the TRUTH that you know!

Start now! Use the **A B C's.**

1. **A**ccept Jesus.

2. **B**elieve and ask God for the Holy Spirit Baptism.

3. **C**ommit yourself to read the four gospel books of Matthew, Mark, Luke, John and also Acts in the Bible. Read them three times in a month.

Now you wear the GIRDLE OF TRUTH. You can say, "Look out termites! You can't invade my house anymore!"

Rasty the Nasty Roach

A large cloth on the kitchen counter covered what looked like several dishes of food. Hungry and tired from the trip to our new church, I relished the idea of a hot meal and was delighted that the ladies had prepared one to welcome us. This was the largest reception we had received. Usually someone was there to greet us and help us unload the trailer or truck but not with a full meal. Sure that we were going to enjoy our term there, I pulled the cover off the food and jumped back at the sight. Swarms of tiny bugs, hundreds of them were attacking our dinner.

"What is this?" I gasped. "Where did they come from?" I was not prepared for an invasion of German roaches.

My husband ran out and bought spray. He sprayed and sprayed, but each morning when I flipped the light switch I faced the same scene. The spray only fed the little pests. They crawled everywhere - the cabinets, drawers, counter tops, I even found a few in the refrigerator. *Now how in the world did they get in there?* Malcolm continued to spray but to no avail.

Finally, when I felt I couldn't take another minute of the intrusion, he called professional exterminators. They came armed with pesticide for that particular roach. Immediately the pests were gone. No longer did they gather around each little crumb that fell on the floor or counter as I cooked or try to beat us to the table when we ate our meals. Why, you would have thought I cooked it for them. We had to rush to fill our plate before they got to the food. Once they were gone they were gone for good. After proper extermination, we never saw them again.

Spiritually, what has invaded your house before you arrived? In other words, what was handed down from former generations? And what treatment will you use to get rid of unwanted spiritual pests?

SECOND ARTICLE OF ARMOR

THE BREASTPLATE OF RIGHTEOUSNESS

And having on the breastplate of righteousness

"Thump. . . thump. . . thump. . ." goes the heart sending life giving blood to all parts of the body. Without this thumping the body dies. There is no life. The breastplate, as we all know, covers this most important part of the body . . . the heart.

We often say that Jesus lives in our heart. When I was a child I learned the song: "Into my heart, into my heart, come into my heart, Lord Jesus. Come in today. Come in to stay. Come into my heart, Lord Jesus." I thought that Jesus came into the thumping part of me, my actual heart. Now I know that the song referrs to the spiritual heart or the center of my being - the part of me that holds salvation. Now I refer to my heart as my inner man.

My inner man holds either good or evil. I can know what is in there by the words my mouth speaks. The Bible tells us, *Out of the abundance of the heart the mouth speaketh (Matthew12:34). For those things that proceed out of the mouth come forth from the heart* (Matthew 15:18).

One cannot hide what is in the heart. The mouth gives it away every time!

Oops! Did I say that?

WHAT'S IN THE HEART

What can our heart hold? Let's look inside and see the things that can be there. Jesus said, *Out of the heart proceed evil thoughts, murders, adulteries, fornications, thefts, false witness, blasphemies (Matthew 15:19).*

Let's dissect these words and see what they mean.

EVIL - poneros - means hurtful, degeneracy, ill, diseased, culpable, derelict, vicious, facinorous, mischief, malice, guilt, the devil, sinners, - bad, evil, grievous, harm, lewd, malicious, wicked.

THOUGHTS - dialogismos - means reasoning, imagination, doubtful, dispute, debate and intellectual rebellions against God.

Did you see any of the things your heart holds as you read the Greek definitions for evil thoughts? Did you know it is wrong to be doubtful? That is an evil thought. We can't reason out everything. We are supposed to trust God not question and doubt Him.

Do all things without murmurings and disputes (Philippians 2:14).

The Amplified version of the Bible says that we are complaining against God instead of circumstances when we murmur and dispute. Thankfulness is not in our heart. God desires for us to have a thankful heart. One that leads us to enter His courts with praise.

MURDERS - phonos - means (to slay), murder, + be slain with, slaughter.

111

Have you ever killed someone's reputation and influence? Have you killed their joy with your gossip? Have you ever hated them so much you could have killed them? "Not as bad as actually doing it," you say. No, but it is still wrong. That's why we need the breastplate of righteousness to keep all these things out of our heart.

THEFTS - klope - means steal. It also comes from a word that means filch or pilfer - steal or thieve in a petty way.

You didn't knowingly walk away with someone's pen did you? Or pick up a fork from a restaurant, thinking, "They won't miss one fork." Maybe you stuck a hotel's towel in your suitcase. If so, could thefts be in your heart?

FALSE WITNESS - pseudomarturia - means untrue testimony.

Do we ever repeat gossip? We hear a rumor and though we are not sure that it is true – we repeat it. To tell an untrue story on someone is as though you took a sack full of feathers to the top of the Empire State Building and dumped them out on a windy day. You could never go down and collect all the feathers and put them back in the bag. Neither can you make it right when you find that the story you told about someone was not true. The lie has already spread beyond collection.

BLASPHEMIES - blasphemia - means vilification, especially against God, evil speaking, railing.

Vilification means to speak ill of.

THE STORY OF A KING AND HIS SON

How often do we speak against and falsely accuse God? It reminds me of the story about a king's young son who left the palace without his father's permission and was on his way to play with a friend. Not taking the time to properly dress for the day he wore only a thin garment, no breastplate or shoes. He had no shield or sword for protection; however he did wear a helmet.

An arch enemy desired to take over the king's throne. The enemy had lost his position in the kingdom and hated the king and his family. Seeing the king's son so ill prepared for the journey, the enemy decided *this is my opportunity to get even with the king. I will attack his son.*

He brutally beat the boy and broke his leg. Since the king's son had worn his helmet, the enemy couldn't hurt his head. The boy could still think and knew that he belonged to the king.

The father missed his son and went out to search for him. He found him by the side of the road, wounded and bleeding. The father took him up in his arms, but the son said, "Father, why did you do this to me?"

The father was surprised at the accusation. "Son, let me help you." He poured ointment into his wounds and bandaged them. After carrying the boy home in his arms the father fed him a wonderful dinner with ice cream for dessert.

The boy said, "Oh, father, I think I know now why you let this happen to me. It's so that you would have a chance to be good to me and show me your love." The father was sad. Didn't the boy understand that the attack came from the family's enemy?

This is the way we treat God. He has an enemy who tries to get even with Him by attacking us. We have equipment to keep ourselves covered but we fail to use it. So often all we have on is the helmet of salvation. When the enemy attacks us, we still know that we are God's child because our head wasn't bashed in, but we don't have the sword of the Spirit which is the Word of God.

We accuse God of causing the attack. Then when He tries to comfort us as a good parent would comfort his child after an attack, we believe that God caused this bad thing to happen for our benefit, when all the time, God is bringing something good out of what the devil did.

Where did we get this doctrine that God does bad things to us to teach us a lesson? Jesus Himself said that *the Holy Ghost will teach you all things. (John 14:26).*

I am not saying that the child could not learn from what happened. He could learn to properly equip himself and get his father's permission before going out, but my point is that the father did not do evil to the child. The enemy did.

Jesus said that He came to give life and that more abundantly. James said that *every good gift and every perfect gift cometh down from the Father of lights, with whom is no variableness neither shadow of turning (James 1:17).*

Jesus said, *I beheld Satan as lightning fall from heaven. Behold I give you power to tread on serpents and scorpions, and over all the power of the enemy; and nothing shall by any means hurt you (Luke 10:19).*

Now when the sun was setting, all they that had any sick with divers diseases brought them unto him; and he laid his hands on every one of them, and healed them. And devils also came out of many (Luke 4:40).

When Jesus was accused of casting out devils by Beelzebub the prince of devils, He said to them, *How can Satan cast out Satan? And if a kingdom be divided against itself, that house cannot stand. And if Satan rise against himself, and be divided he cannot stand, but hath an end (Mark 3:22-26).*

By the same token, if God be divided against Himself He cannot stand. If He puts sickness, accidents, sorrows, and diseases on us and then turns around and takes them off, He is divided against Himself.

Some Christians act like Jesus came to give us sickness and diseases and the devil came to take them off. People, we have it backwards. When will we stop accusing God?

Mark said that *Jesus ordained twelve that they should be with him, and that he might send them forth to preach, with power to heal sicknesses, and to cast out devils (Mark 3:14-15).*

Luke tells us in chapter ten that He sent out seventy. He told them to heal the sick and preach the kingdom of heaven is at hand. They came back rejoicing that the devils were subject to them through Jesus' name.

If Jesus sent them out to heal the sick, then why do Christians think that God put the sickness on them? He would be divided against Himself. Jesus said that He came to do the Father's will. He healed every sick person who came to Him.

The reason our doctrine has strayed so far away from what Jesus taught is because we are not reading what Jesus said. We are reading most of the time in the Old Testament or in the epistles. Not many are preaching what Jesus said. As a church, we claim that the New Testament is our only rule of government. Why don't we preach and practice what Jesus said and did? We would have to stop blaming and accusing God if we did. Jesus came to show us the Father. Everywhere He went He healed the sick and cast out devils. Never once did He put sickness or disease on a person.

He was criticized for healing and casting out devils. Once in the synagogue when He had cast out an unclean spirit, the crowd was astonished. They said, *What thing is this? What new doctrine is this? For with authority commandeth he even the unclean spirits, and they do obey him (Mark 1:27).*

What is in your heart? Do you see Jesus as a healer or as one who puts sickness on people? Do you see Him as the deliverer of evil spirits or one who puts them on a person? Let's see Him for the healer and deliverer that He is and stop accusing God.

Don't let the pest of accusation against God remain in your life.

THE WORKS OF THE FLESH

Paul talks about another list of sins in the book of Galatians. He calls them the works of the flesh. They are more pests who try to invade our lives.

Now the works of the flesh are manifest, which are these; adultery, fornication, uncleanness, lasciviousness, idolatry, witchcraft, hatred, variance, emulations, wrath, strife, seditions, heresies, envyings, murders, drunkenness, revellings, and such like: of the which I tell you before, as I have also told you in time past, that they which do such things shall not inherit the kingdom of God (Galatians5:19-21).

They that are Christ's have crucified the flesh with the affections and lusts (Galatians 5:24).

Did you know that all these things are in the heart of the unrighteous? When we come to Jesus and confess our sins, the Bible says, *He is faithful and just to forgive us of our sins and to cleanse us from all unrighteousness (I John 1:9).* Then we put on the breastplate so these evil pests cannot get back in.

Since we are supposed to crucify the flesh and get rid of these works of the flesh, let's examine each one and see of what they consist.

ADULTERY - Greek moicheuo - means adultery. Hebrew word na'nph also means adultery. Both words mean to break wedlock. We talked about this in the last chapter. It is still a sin to commit adultery which means to have sex with someone other than your marriage partner. One of the Ten Commandments is thou shalt not commit adultery.

FORNICATION - Four words from the Bible that are translated fornication are:

1. Zanah - a Hebrew word that means - highly fed and therefore wanton (wanton means - wild, unchaste, purposeless, undisciplined): to commit adultery, whore. Also to commit idolatry (worship other gods).

2. *Taznuwth* - harlotry, idolatry, fornication and whoredom.

3. *Porneia* - a New Testament word that means - harlotry, includes adultery and incest.

4. *Ekporneuo* - to be utterly unchaste give self over to fornication.

Jude 7 says, *Giving themselves over to fornication.*

UNCLEANNESS - Two words in the Old Testament for uncleanness are:

1. *Niddah* - which means impurity, especially personally (ministration) or moral (idolatry, incest).

2. *Tum'ah* - to be foul or morally contaminated. Defile self, pollute self, and make self unclean.

118

In the New Testament, the word is *akatharsia*. It also means impurity, physically or morally.

In chapter one, we talked about Romans 1: 24. It says that God gave the people up to uncleanness through the lusts of their *hearts*. Then He describes the act of the homosexual as uncleanness

GOOD NEWS FOR THE UNCLEAN

Romans 6:19 says, *For as ye have yielded your members servants to uncleanness and to iniquity unto iniquity; even so now yield your members servants to righteousness unto holiness. For when ye were the servants of sin, ye were free from righteousness* (Romans 6:19b-20).

He said in the next verse that you are now ashamed of those things and that the end of those things is death. *But now being made free from sin and become servants to God, ye have your fruit unto holiness (or righteousness) and the end everlasting life. For, the wages of sin is death, but the gift of God is eternal life through Jesus Christ our Lord (Romans 6:22-23).*

LASCIVIOUSNESS - *Aselgeia* - means licentiousness, filthy, lasciviousness, wantonness. *Lasciviousness is the promoting or partaking of that which tends to produce lewd emotions, anything tending to foster sex sin and lust. That is why many worldly pleasures have to be avoided by the Christian - so that lasciviousness may not be committed. * Dake

119

The type of clothes we wear is significant also. Revealing and seductive clothes can promote lewd emotions and stir lust.

IDOLATRY - eidoloatreia - means image worship. Idolatry includes anything on which affections are passionately set; extravagant admiration of the heart. *

Are we bringing idols into our homes? I see many images of so called gods prevalent in homes today. I shudder to think of the consequences. God said, *The graven images of their gods shall ye burn with fire: thou shalt not desire the silver or gold that is on them, nor take it unto thee, lest thou be snared therein; for it is an abomination to the Lord thy God. Neither shalt thou bring an abomination into thine house lest thou be a cursed thing like it: but thou shall utterly detest it, and thou shalt utterly abhor it; for it is a cursed thing (Deuteornomy.7:25).*

WITCHCRAFT - pharmakeia - means sorcery, practice of dealing with evil spirits, magical incantations, casting spells and charms upon one by means of drugs and potions of various kinds. Enchants were used to inflict evil, pains, hatred, sufferings, and death, or to bring good health, love and other blessing. *

God said, *there shall not be found among you anyone that maketh his son or daughter to pass through the fire, or that useth divinations, or an observer of times, or an enchanter, or a witch, or a charmer, or a consulter with familiar spirits, or a wizard, or a necromancer. For all that do these things are an abomination unto the Lord (Deuteronomy 18:10-12).*

HATRED - echtbra - means enmity, bitter dislike, abhorrence, malice, and ill-will against anyone; tendency to hold grudges or be angry at someone. *

Uh oh. Do you wish something evil on someone? Or hold a grudge? Are you bitter or angry towards a person? That's hatred!

VARIANCE - eris - means dissections, discord, quarreling, debating, and disputes.*

How about quarreling? When was the last time you did that?

EMULATIONS - zeloi - means envies, jealousies; striving to excel at the expense of another, seeking to surpass and outdo others; uncurbed rivalry spirit in religion, business, society, and other fields of endeavor. *

This one hurts! Are you jealous or envious? Not glad when others prosper? Do you try to outdo others even in the religious world?

WRATH - *thumos* – means - indignation and fierceness, turbulent passions; domestic and civil turmoil; rage; determined and lasting anger. *

Lasting anger stays and stays. The Bible says, *Don't let the sun go down on your wrath (Ephesians 4:26)*. Get over your mad spell before dark.

STRIFE - eritheia - means contention; disputations; janglings; strife about words; angry contentions; contests for superiority or advantage; strenuous endeavor to equal or pay back in kind the wrongs done to one. *

121

Are you planning to get even for a wrong done to you? Drop it. It will only hurt you. When you *get even* with someone, you lower yourself to their level.

SEDITIONS - *dichostasia* - means divisions, parties and factions, popular disorder; stirring up strife in religion, government, home, or any other place. *

Do you stir things up? Do you cause trouble at home or work or where ever? Stop it! Get it out of your heart.

HERESIES - *hairesis* - means a choice, i.e. a party or disunion, sect. It is a doctrinal view or belief at variance with the norm. Evil appears when sound doctrine is rejected. *

Do you believe the truth? Stick with sound doctrine, the doctrine of the Bible.

ENVYINGS- phthonoi - means pain, ill-will, and jealousy at the good fortune or blessing of another; the most base of all degrading and disgraceful passions.*

The Bible says, *Rejoice with them that do rejoice and weep with them that weep (Romans 12:15).* We should be glad when people are blessed and rejoice with them.

It also says, *Rejoice not when thine enemy falleth, and let not thine heart be glad when he stumbleth; Lest the Lord see it, and it displease him, and he turn away his wrath from him (Proverbs 24:17).*

MURDERS - phonoi - means to kill to spoil or mar the happiness of another; hatred.*

122

Whosoever hateth his brother is a murderer; and ye know that no murderer hath eternal life abiding in him (1 John 3:15).

DRUNKENNESS - methai - means living intoxicated; a slave to drink, drinking bouts.*

How many children have suffered untold agony because of a father or mother's drunkenness?

REVELLINGS - komoi - means rioting, lascivious and boisterous feastings, with obscene music, and other sinful activities; pleasures; carousings.*

It sounds like we shouldn't hang out in a dive or juke joint. And how about the music we listen to?

There are four divisions of these 17 sins that live in the heart.

1 - 4 are sins of lust.

5 - 6 are sins of impiety and superstition.

7 - 15 are sins of temper.

16 - 17 are sins of appetite - eating and drinking. *

* Taken from Dake

WHAT IS RIGHTEOUSNESS?

It is not self-righteousness. *Our righteousness is as filthy rags (Isaiah 64:6). There is none righteous, no, not one (Romans 3:10).*

The breastplate of righteousness protects us from the sins of the heart we discussed above.

RIGHTEOUSNESS - dikaiosune - means justification. It is taken from dikaios meaning innocent, holy, just, meet, right (-eous) which comes from dlischurizomal and means asseverate-confidently (constantly) affirm. This word comes from ischus meaning forcible - boisterous, mighty, powerful, strong, valiant.

I understand from this definition that when you put on the breastplate of righteousness you are declaring or affirming boisterously that through the blood of Jesus you are justified – just- as-if-I'd- never-done-it. This gives you strength and makes you mighty and powerful!

TO RECEIVE RIGHTEOUSNESS ONE MUST:

1. Seek God. *Seek first the kingdom of God and His righteousness (Matthew 6:33).*

2. Know that Jesus Christ is the *righteousness of God (Romans 3:19-26).*

3. Understand that our righteousness comes from Jesus. *For He made him who knew no sin to be sin for us, that we might become the righteousness of God in* Him *(II Cor. 5:21).*

4. Know that it comes by faith. *Even the righteousness of God, through faith in Jesus Christ, to all and on all who believe (Romans 3:22).*

HOW DO I PUT ON THE BREASTPLATE OF RIGHTEOUSNESS?

There are four steps. They are:

1. Examine your heart.

As you read the list of sins of the heart did you see yourself? If you wanted to skip over one of the definitions go back and read it again. Usually we want to skip the part of the Word that reveals our shortcomings. That is the one we need to read again.

2. Ask the Holy Spirit to search your heart.

If you don't see unrighteousness in your heart, ask the Holy Spirit to turn on His light and reveal anything hidden. Satan tries to hide the truth from us. It's much easier to see other's faults than to see our own.

3. When you find it, confess it.

Pray and ask God to forgive and cleanse the secret sins of the heart. He will be glad to do it. Ask the Holy Spirit to be your helper to keep your heart clean.

Let's pray now:

Father God,

I desire a clean heart. I have seen and confess (put your sins here). Reveal any secret sins that live there. Forgive and cleanse me of all sin and create within me a pure heart. Set a guard on my heart so that these things cannot find their way inside again.

David prayed these prayers:

Let the words of my mouth and the meditation of my heart; be acceptable in thy sight, O Lord, my strength and my redeemer (Psalm 19:14).

Create in me a clean heart, O God; and renew a right spirit within me (Psalm 51:10).

4. Read the list of sins of the heart daily for a week. Become familiar with them. Notice if you commit any. Turn those sins over to the Lord. Pray David's prayers daily.

YOU ARE NOW WEARING THE BREASTPLATE OF RIGHTEOUSNESS.

The cleansing power of the Word of God has destroyed the invading army of nasty roaches that attacked your flesh. Now the righteousness of your heart is protected.

Honey Bees Are Not Always Sweet

Honey Bees promise sweetness in life. That wasn't the case when a colony built their hive under my friend Mary's mobile home. They never made it inside the house, but as they came and went, their buzzing and humming was nerve wracking. The constant threat that one could fly inside the moment Mary opened her door created fear. A bee's sting at the least is painful and at the most to those who are allergic - deadly.

Sometimes Satan offers sweetness, pleasure, a good time if we only let him in. When we refuse, he builds a colony of demons right under us and threatens to destroy our peace. He causes arguments, strife, disagreements, and feuds. He makes us think when someone does us wrong that revenge would be sweet – like honey.

Don't be fooled. If you let that demon in, his sting may be lethal. We are all allergic to sin.

The hive under Mary's house grew bigger and more aggressive until the next door neighbor complained. Then one of the bees flew right at Mary as she walked in her yard. She called an exterminator. He was not allowed to spray them as bees are a protected species.

He tried to find a bee keeper to remove them, but no one wanted to mess with a strange colony of bees.

Finally the exterminator did the usual bug spraying around the house and succeeded in making about sixty of the bees very upset. The workers went into a rage, and swarmed in angry circles. After all it was their job to protect the queen, the honey and the youngsters. They followed the exterminator around until he finally turned the nozzle on them. Knowing the communication habits of bees, he hoped they would notify the rest of the hive of danger in the area so they would vacate.

The bees must have worked all night packing up because early the next morning Mary's son, whose bedroom was directly over the hive, heard a funny noise.

When Mary got up, the hive was empty except for a few really mad bees that remained behind to protect the nest. Mary and her son had to spray them or get stung. Next they had to remove the nest so the swarm wouldn't come back or call on other bees to make their home there.

Like these bees who would return if not stopped, evil spirits will try to come back in once a life is delivered. Jesus gave us a warning in the Bible in Matthew 12:43-45. He tells about an unclean spirit that leaves a man, wanders in dry places and then returns to the house he left. He finds it empty, swept and decorated. He goes out and brings seven more spirits that are worse than he to inhabit the clean house. Jesus said that the last state of that man is worse than the first.

Be aware. If you are delivered of evil spirits, fill your house with God's Word, prayer and praise to God. Go to church and stay close to Jesus. Satan does not give up easily. We battle all of our lives to maintain the victories we have won.

THIRD ARTICLE OF ARMOR

SHOES OF PEACE

And your feet shod with the preparation
of the gospel of peace

A woman saw in a vision an army of women dressed in armor. They all wore boots that came to their knees - silver boots. Prepared for walking, or was it running? They were ready to chase the enemy. We do not run from him, he runs from us. *Resist the devil and he will flee from you (James 4:7).*

God wants our feet ready to carry the gospel of peace. Remember as a child the feeling when we first pulled off our socks and shoes to go barefoot for the summer? At first, we had to walk lightly and tip toe around because our feet were tender. We didn't get much done. Going outside we stepped on a sandspur. "Ouch!" we cried. "That hurts." When it was time to go shopping mama said, "Put on your shoes." She knew we couldn't keep up with her barefooted.

God is saying to us today, "Put on your shoes. I want you to carry the gospel of peace for Me."

When someone steps on our toes and hurts our feelings we may cry "Ouch!" as we did when the sandspurs hurt, but with the shoes of peace on we don't pay as much attention to what others do to us. Instead we want to help them by taking them the gospel.

PEACE - eirene means by implication prosperity: one, peace, quietness, rest, plus set at one again.

It sounds like God wants us to make up with whom we are out of touch becoming as one again to produce quietness in our emotions, our soul. When we are not in peace with others, our life is in turmoil. Nothing goes right. We can't sleep.

Jesus wants to show us how to live wearing the shoes of peace. We read that Jesus came *to guide our feet into the way of peace (Luke 1:79).*

Jesus said, *Have salt in yourselves and have peace one with another (Mark 9:50 b).*

Paul said, *Let us therefore follow after the things which make for peace, and things wherewith one may edify another (Romans 14:19).*

Edify means to build up. Are we interested in building someone else up or do we just want our own way? When we want our own way we are hard to live with. We are not peaceful.

God is not the author of confusion but of peace (I Corinthians 14:33). Who is the author of turmoil? It has to be Satan. When we cause confusion in our family or church or on the job, guess who we are working for? That's right, Satan. But when we create peace we are doing God's work.

Finally, brethren, farewell. Be perfect, be of good comfort, be of one mind, live in peace, and the God of love and peace shall be with you (II Corinthians 13:11).

Follow peace with all men (Hebrews 12:14).

And the fruit of righteousness is sown in peace of them that make peace (James 3:18).

We must have peace in our own minds. Spiritual quietness comes from Jesus. He said:

Peace I leave with you, my peace I give unto you (John 14:27).

These things have I spoken unto you that in me ye might have peace (John 16:33).

Paul said, *And the peace of God which passeth all understanding, shall keep your hearts and minds through Christ Jesus (Philippians 4:7).*

ANN'S CROWN OF PEACE

The ladies conducted Wednesday morning prayer meetings in one of the churches where my husband was pastor. In spite of the fact that Ann, a woman of the church, attended each week, she remained high strung and edgy. One morning she arrived obviously upset.

"I am all to pieces! I am so nervous I can't stand myself another minute," she said. "Please pray for me."

I laid hands on her forehead as several ladies gathered around. I heard myself pray, "Lord, crown Ann with peace." What a surprise! I never expected that to come out of my mouth.

Ann began to cry and praise God. Finally, she managed to say, "When you prayed it felt like someone placed a crown on my head. Something warm ran from my head all the way to my feet and spread through my body. I am not trembling. All of my life I have been so nervous. Ever since I can remember from the time I was a young girl I felt my insides shaking. It's gone! I have the peace of God."

We all enjoyed a time of rejoicing, thanking God for His peace. Later, Ann testified she was still calm and peaceful in her body and mind.

MY DREAM

Several years ago, I dreamed that I was hired as a waitress. On the way to the new job, I looked down and saw two big spots on my uniform. *It's probably coffee. The spots will dry before I get to work. If they leave a stain I'll hide them with my apron. Nobody will know.*

When I arrived at the work site, I looked at my feet and realized they were bare. That seemed strange. I found my shoes, put them on, went into the restaurant and found the tables full. On approaching the first one, I saw a woman from another country with long dark hair. "May I help you?"

"Yes," she said, "I have a problem with my lungs. At times I can hardly breathe." Her answer surprised me. *I thought I was here to serve food.*

"I know someone who can help you," I said and told her about Jesus who can save the soul and heal the body. Then I laid hands on her forehead and prayed for her healing. She accepted the prayer and my dream ended.

On awakening, I was excited about the ministry but troubled by missing shoes and spots on my garment. I supposed I was not ready to minister because the Bible says that God wants a holy people without spot or wrinkle. I knew the two stains represented something hidden within - something that kept me from walking in the gospel of peace and ministering to my full potential.

"What were the two spots?" I asked God. I heard in my spirit - jealousy and resentment. Two sins we studied in the last chapter - hidden sins of the heart.

I attended a women's prayer meeting that morning at my friend Janie's house, confessed the dream and received prayer. God set me free from the jealousy and resentment. With my heart cleansed of bad feelings towards others, I could put on my shoes of peace. Now I was ready to minister.

The following week at the prayer meeting, I met and ministered to the woman I saw in my dream. She had long dark hair, was from another country, and said the same words, "I have something wrong with my lungs. At times I can hardly breathe"

Because I had confessed the hidden sins of my heart, I ministered to her and she was saved and healed. Happy that God had revealed my sins, I put on my shoes of peace.

What about your feet? Are they ready to take you in paths of reconciliation with God, and others, so that you can make people as 'one with God,' helping them find peace?

HOW DO YOU PUT ON THE SHOES OF PEACE?

There are four steps. They are:

1. **Be at peace with God**. Are you accusing him falsely? Blaming Him for things that Satan has done? If so, apologize to Him.

2. **Make peace with others.** Are you at odds with someone? Holding a grudge? Be honest.

> a. Go to them and apologize.
>
> b. If you can't reach them write a letter.
>
> Everyone may not accept your apology. Be prepared to forgive them anyway.
>
> c. If the person died, write them a letter, read it out loud as if they were there. Destroy the letter and let go of your bad feelings against them.

3. **Allow God to put His peace inside of you.**

4. **Pray for peace.**

Dear God,

I need You. Someone has hurt my feelings, (or stolen my money, slapped me, raped me, stole my husband, left me, wrecked my car, took my inheritance, you name it.)

I am willing to forgive (name them), but I am having a hard time doing it. Will You forgive through me? Please, give me the peace of God that passes understanding. Amen.

Now that you are wearing the SHOES OF PEACE you are able to be an effective witness of the gospel. You are ready to minister to others. No more tormenting bees buzzing around in your emotions, causing strife and division.

Bees be gone!

ARNIE THE ARMADILLO

My friend, Vern, loved working in her new yard, planting colorful flowers and beautiful bushes. She created gardens and paths lined with delicate shrubs and blossoms spending days of digging, planting, sorting and arranging, trimming, and watering. In the cool of the day she loved to walk on the paths admiring God's handiwork that her toil had arranged. She felt God's presence.

Overnight, all of her hard work was undermined. Arnie the armadillo burrowed underground and went from plant to plant uprooting and destroying all of her beautiful flowers and shrubs. When she took her coffee out the next morning to sip and enjoy nature, her yard was a shamble. Tears flowed as disappointment nearly overwhelmed her.

Vern was a fighter – a godly warrior. When the shock wore off, she dried her eyes, put on her work clothes and replanted every one of the uprooted flowers and bushes. This time she decided to do something to keep Arnie the armadillo out. With her husband's help, she stationed little garden fences up and down the paths and around the flower beds.

Arnie and his buddies disregarded the fences. Again the next morning all the plants lay on top of the ground.

Vern replanted and tried a different approach – traps. That didn't work either. Day after day the process was repeated. Each time Vern tried something new. Night after night the attackers invaded and destroyed. She spent lots of money and plenty of sweat and tears. It all seemed in vain.

Have you ever tried to remedy the effect of Satan and his cohorts? You may have spent money you couldn't afford to get help for a troubled child, doctors for a disease, psychiatrist for a sick mind, and rehab for a drug or alcohol problem, or bail for someone in jail, etc. It seems like a never ending list.

Like Vern, you had worked to create a beautiful life for your family, nurturing relationships, tending to business affairs, creating harmony and peace with relatives and then overnight it's demolished. Your world crashed around you. You felt like the battle would go on forever.

It's all part of Satan's plan to destroy you. Remember Jesus said that Satan came to kill, steal and destroy. Don't let him! You are a warrior! Fight him with all you have.

Not long ago, I visited Vern and admired her beautiful flowers and bushes. "I see you finally got the best of the armadillos," I said.

"Not really," Vern replied, "I just keep fighting."

Keep fighting! Jesus won the victory at Calvary, but we have to keep fighting until Satan is cast into the pit. We maintain our ground by faith until we see it.

FOURTH ARTICLE OF ARMOR

THE SHIELD OF FAITH

Above all, taking the shield of faith

The church prayed again for much needed rain. A little girl, unable to attend the services before that day, grabbed her umbrella from the closet and headed for the church. Upon her arrival the pastor said, "Sally it hasn't rained in weeks. Why did you bring your umbrella?"

She answered, "I thought we were meeting to pray for rain."

FAITH is knowing. The little girl didn't wonder if it would rain; she knew the Bible says that whatsoever we ask in His name we receive. She prepared to receive. That's faith.

Faith doesn't hope or think. Faith knows. Faith comes by hearing, hearing by the Word of God. You have read the Bible. You know what God did in the past. You know His heart, mind, and will. You know what He said He will do. You believe it. You know that He keeps His word. You have faith.

I used to wonder how to have faith. I closed my eyes and tried real hard to believe and have faith. When I began to read the Word of God each day and talk to Him in prayer, I no longer struggled to have faith. I knew God through His Word. I knew him through talking to Him in prayer. I believed Him because I knew Him.

You don't wonder before you sit down in a chair if the chair will hold you. You don't wonder if the light will come on when you flip the switch. You don't question if your car will start when you turn the key. You KNOW that these things will take place. That's faith.

I don't understand how electricity works but I know that it does. I have faith in electricity. I believe that when I press the button, electricity will flow through my television. and I will see a picture. I don't know how but I know it will. I have faith.

I don't understand everything about God but I know that He answers prayer. I know that He loves me. I know that Jesus died to save me. I have faith.

FAITH from the Greek means assurance, belief, believe, fidelity. Assurance means that you are sure of something. It means to remove all possible doubt. This goes back to knowing. Faith is knowing.

SATAN'S FIERY DARTS

"Above all, taking the shield of faith, wherewith ye shall be able to quench all the fiery darts of the wicked" (Ephesians 6:16).

The *wicked* refers to Satan, the evil one, the devil. In John 10:10, Jesus says that the thief comes to kill, steal and destroy but Jesus comes to bring abundant life.

I believe that everything evil comes from the devil. Everything good comes from God. There are only two powers - good and evil. It is a very simple concept.

A CHILD'S SERMON

My 5 year old granddaughter stood in my den one afternoon and for about 15 minutes preached this sermon:

"There is only good and evil," she said. "On the one hand," she raised her right hand out to her right side, "there is good. On the other hand," she held out her left hand lower than the right hand, "is evil. Everything good," (right hand out,) "is of God. And everything evil," (left hand out,) "is of the devil. If on the one hand you choose God," (right hand extended) "then you will do good but if on the other hand" (left hand extended) "you choose the devil then you will do evil. You have a choice. You can choose God and be good or you can choose the way of the devil and do bad. If you choose good," (right hand out and up,) "then you will have a good life and things will go good for you. If you choose the devil," (left hand out lower,) "then you will have a bad life and bad will come to you. If you choose God and good when you die you will go to heaven but if you choose bad and the devil then when you die you will go to hell. Which do you want? God or the devil? Good or evil? Heaven or hell? It's up to you."

The anointing of God flowed through Michelle as she continued her message for several minutes, holding out her right hand each time she spoke of good, God, or heaven and holding out her left hand lower each time she spoke of evil, the devil, or hell. She spoke truth that was beyond the wisdom of a five- year-old child.

Let's talk more about the Scripture *Above all, taking the shield of faith, wherewith ye shall be able to quench all the fiery darts of the wicked (Ephesians 6:16).*

TAKE THE D OFF OF DEVIL. ALL THAT'S LEFT IS EVIL. HE USES THE D TO CREATE - D - DARTS

This Scripture says that fiery darts come from the devil. He loves to throw them at the child of God. Notice if you take the letter D off of the front of Devil all that is left is evil. Most of his evil darts start with the letter D just like his name. I call them D-Darts. The first one I'd like to talk about is:

DISAPPOINTMENT

Things didn't turn out the way you expected. You are disappointed. It is a sad feeling. You question, "Why did things happen this way?" You expected more. You are let down, your self-esteem wounded. "What did I do wrong? Why can't I ever do anything right?"

This leads to the next dart,

DOUBT

You wonder if God really loves you. If He did, then why did things go wrong? Disappointment increases as doubt speaks, "God didn't hear your prayer. Will He ever?" Doubt makes you susceptible to the next dart:

DISCOURAGEMENT

What's the use in trying? Where is God? You can't feel Him like you used to. Has He left you? Why doesn't the Bible seem clearer? It used to make more sense than it does now. You feel numb and it's hard to concentrate. Am I really saved? I wouldn't feel like this if I was. The devil's

142

bombardment of discouragement leads to the next dart,

DESPONDENCY

Now you wallow in self-pity. "Just can't get it right, can you?" Satan whispers. "Others are doing good but not you. See how everyone else is blessed. What is it with you? Loser!"

The mud bog of despondency opens the door to

DESPAIR

Sinking deeper into the bog, you reach despair. All seems hopeless. There is no way out of your situation. What are you to do? Drowning in the river of despair, your immune system weakens and you receive another D-dart.

DEPRESSION

Every day is like the day before. You're not getting anywhere. None of your goals were met. What's happened to your life? You always thought that you would accomplish more. You're a total failure. With this sickness you'll never get your projects done. Why get out of bed? What's the point. Is life even worth living? "Why don't you end it all and get out of your misery," Satan whispers. This dart often makes way for:

DISEASE

It hits when you least expect it. You're sick with an incurable disease. Even if it is curable it takes a long time to get over. Days drag by. Life is set on a shelf. Nothing is normal. Your whole life is interrupted from the flow of things. Hit with the dart of disease can lead to

DEATH

The absence of life. The end of one type of existence and the beginning of another. There are different spirits of death:

Abortion - the death of a baby

Discord - the death of a friendship

Divorce- the death of a marriage

Disease- the death of good health

Death stinks. And death is final.

Other D-Darts are:

Decay - Deception - Decrease – Distract - Defeat – Distress - Disillusionment - Dismay – Disgrace - Disaster.

The devil's list is inexhaustible. You may be able to add some of your own darts that the devil has thrown at you.

GOOD NEWS

The good news is that the shield of faith will quench ALL the fiery darts of the devil. Not some or a few, but ALL. These darts hurt and leave scars if left in too long but faith will quench them. When Satan throws the dart of disappointment, put up the shield of faith by quoting the Scripture "I am more than a conqueror through Him who loved me and gave Himself for me." When Satan says "You can't do anything right," tell him "I can do all things through Christ who strengthens me."

When it seems that you are drowning in despair, do what Jesus said in Matthew "Speak to the mountain and command it to be cast into the sea." Then sit back and watch it move out of your life.

When disease hits quench that dart with the shield of faith that says, "With His stripes I am healed."

FAITH

Faith begins with F. Other good words that start with F are, Forward, Friend, Find Favor, Fortitude, Founded, Firm Footing, and Fight. Yes you can go FORWARD and find FAVOR. You can have Friends and be Fortified while Founded on a Firm Footing. Yes you can Fight the good Fight of Faith with the shield of Faith and quench all the fiery darts of the devil!

SHIELD

God spoke to Abraham in a vision. *Fear not Abram: I am thy shield and thy exceeding great reward (Genesis 15:1).* We know that a shield is a piece of armor held in front of a person that protects him.

God said to Israel, *Happy art thou, O Israel: who is like unto thee, O people saved by the Lord, the shield of thy help, and who is the sword of thy excellency (Deuteronomy 33:29)!*

Shields in that time were made large enough for a man to stand behind and be completely covered. It is said that Goliath's shield was so large that another man had to

145

carry it for him. It weighed 30 pounds. I believe that God is still big enough to cover us completely in every situation. Faith in Him is our shield. Faith will protect us from all the fiery darts of the devil.

HOW DO I USE THE SHIELD OF FAITH?

1. READ, READ, READ, THE BIBLE. Faith comes by hearing and hearing by the Word of God. If you read Matthew, Mark, Luke, John and Acts three times in a month as you were asked to do in the first chapter assignment, you are on your way to having GREAT FAITH - faith that will cover you completely. Keep reading.

2. MEMORIZE SCRIPTURE - especially faith building scriptures. Print them on 3x5 index cards. Place one on your bathroom mirror and read it each time you wash your hands or brush your teeth. Change it weekly or when you have memorized it. If you memorize one a week that's fifty-two in a year. Not an impossible goal, but one that will increase your shield of faith.

Memorize the Scriptures below to drive out doubt and increase faith.

DO YOU DOUBT YOUR SALVATION? *MEMORIZE:*

For God so loved the world, that he gave his only begotten son, that whosoever believeth in him should not perish, but have everlasting life (John 3:16).

That if thou shalt confess with thy mouth the Lord Jesus, and shalt believe in thine heart that God hath raised him from the dead, thou shalt be saved (Romans 10:9).

For with the heart man believeth unto righteousness; and with the mouth confession is made unto salvation (Roans10:10).

For whosoever shall call upon the name of the Lord shall be saved (Romans 10:13).

So then faith cometh by hearing, and hearing by the word of God. (Romans 10:17).

If we say that we have no sin, we deceive ourselves, and the truth is not in us (I John 1:8).

If we confess our sins, he is faithful and just to forgive us our sins, and to cleanse us from all unrighteousness (I John 1:9).

If we say that we have not sinned, we make him a liar, and his word is not in us (I John 1:10).

My little children, these things write I unto you, that ye sin not. And if any man sin, we have an advocate with the Father, Jesus Christ the righteous; And he is the propitiation for our sins: and not for ours only, but also for the sins of the whole world (I John 2:1-2).

And hereby we do know that we know him, if we keep his commandments (I John 2:3).

He that saith, I know him, and keepeth not his commandments, is a liar, and the truth is not in him (I John 2:4).

He that saith he is in the light, and hateth his brother, is in darkness even until now (I John 2:9).

He that loveth his brother abideth in the light, and there is none occasion of stumbling in him (I John 2:10).

Behold, what manner of love the Father hath bestowed upon us, that we should be called the sons of God; therefore the world knoweth us not, because it knew him not (I John 3: 1).

Beloved now are we the sons of God, and it doth not yet appear what we shall be; but we know that, when he shall appear, we shall be like him; for we shall see him as he is (I John 3:2).

IF YOU DOUBT HEALING MEMORIZE:

Heal me, O Lord, and I shall be healed; save me, and I shall be saved: for thou art my praise (Jeremiah 17:14).

And His fame went throughout all Syria: and they brought unto him all sick people that were taken with divers diseases and torments, and those which were possessed with devils, and those which were lunatic, and those that had the palsy; and he healed them (Matthew 4:24).

And behold, there came a leper and worshipped him saying, Lord, if thou wilt, thou canst make me clean. And Jesus put forth his hand, and touched him, saying, I will; be thou clean. And immediately his leprosy was cleansed (Matthew 8:2-3).

And Jesus saith unto him, I will come and heal him (Matthew 8:7).

And Jesus said unto the centurion, Go thy way; and as thou hast believed, so be it done unto thee. And his servant was healed in the selfsame hour (Matthew 8:13).

And when Jesus was come into Peter's house, he saw his wife's mother laid, and sick of a fever. And he touched her hand, and the fever left her: and she arose, and ministered unto them (Matthew 8:14-15).

When the even was come, they brought unto him many that were possessed with devils: and he cast out the spirits with his word, and healed all that were sick: That it might be fulfilled which was spoken by Esaias the prophet, saying, "Himself took our infirmities, and bare our sicknesses" (Matthew 8:16-17).

And when he had called unto him his twelve disciples, he gave them power against unclean spirits, to cast them out, and to heal all manner of sickness and all manner of disease (Matthew 10:1).

And as ye go, preach saying, "The kingdom of heaven is at hand." Heal the sick, cleanse the lepers, raise the dead, cast out devils: freely ye have received, freely give. (Matthew 10:8).

Great multitudes followed him, and he healed them all (Matthew 12:15 b).

Then was brought unto him one possessed with a devil, blind, and dumb: and he healed him, insomuch that the blind and dumb both spake and saw (Matthew 12:22).

And Jesus went forth, and saw a great multitude, and was moved with compassion toward them, and he healed their sick (Matthew 14:14).

How God anointed Jesus of Nazareth with the Holy Ghost and with power; who went about doing good and healing all that were oppressed of the devil: for God was with him (Acts 10:38).

Is any sick among you? Let him call for the elders of the church; and let them pray over him, anointing him with oil in the name of the Lord and the prayer of faith shall save the sick, and the Lord shall raise him up; and if he has committed sins, they shall be forgiven him (James 5:14-15).

And the blind and the lame came to him in the temple; and he healed them (Matthew 21:14).

And he healed many that were sick of divers diseases, and cast out many devils; and suffered not the devils to speak, because they knew him (Mark 1:34).

For he had healed many; insomuch that they pressed upon him for to touch him, as many as had plagues. And unclean spirits, when they saw him, fell down before him, and cried, saying, Thou art the Son of God (Mark 3:10-11).

And he said unto her; Daughter, thy faith hath made thee whole; go in peace, and be whole of thy plague (Mark 5:34).

And the power of the Lord was present to heal them Luke 5:17 c).

And they (disciples) cast out many devils, and anointed with oil many that were sick, and healed them (Mark 6:13).

Confess your faults one to another, and pray one for another, that ye may be healed. The effectual fervent prayer of a righteous man availeth much (James 5:16).

But he was wounded for our transgressions, he was bruised for our iniquities: the chastisement of our peace was upon him; and with his stripes we are healed (Isaiah 53:5).

Who his own self bare our sins in his own body on the tree that we, being dead to sins, should live unto righteousness: by whose stripes ye were healed (I Peter 2:24).

So Abraham prayed unto God: and God healed Abimelech, and his wife, and his maidservants; and they bare children (Genesis 20:17).

I am the Lord that healeth thee (Exodus 15:26).

He sent his word and healed them (Psalm 107:20).

But unto you that fear (reverence) my name shall the Sun of righteousness arise with healing in his wings (Malachi 4:2).

O Lord my God, I cried unto thee, and thou hast healed me (Ps. 30:2).

ASK THINGS OF GOD AND RECEIVE THEM.

DO YOU DOUBT? READ:

Ask, and it shall be given you: seek, and ye shall find: knock, and it shall be opened unto you: For every one that asketh receiveth; and he that seeketh findeth, and to him that knocketh it shall be opened (Matthew 7:7).

If ye ask anything in my name I will do it (John 14:14).

If ye abide in me, and my words abide in you, ye shall ask what ye will, and it shall be done unto you (John 15:7).

Ask and ye shall receive that your joy may be full (John 16:24 b).

Beloved, if our heart condemn us not, then have we confidence toward God (I John 3:21).

And whatsoever we ask, we receive of him, because we keep his commandments, and do those things that are pleasing in His sight (I John 3:22).

USE THE SHIELD OF FAITH

Are you using the shield of faith by holding it up against all the fiery darts of the devil? That means you are quoting scripture to him and Satan can't reach you.

He won't be like Arnie the Armidillo running around uprooting all the beautiful things in your life. No. When you learn to use the scripture as a weapon, and the shield of faith for protection, Satan will run from you!

152

Thank God for the Shield of Faith.

THERE'S A RAT IN THE HOUSE. GET THE TRAP!

I awoke with a start, the dream fresh in my mind. *What was that about?* In the dream, a huge rat ate everything in sight in my house. Room by room it ate all the furniture: couch, beds, dressers. I watched as it devoured the whole dining room table. I gasped as it ate all the decorations right off the walls: pictures, sconces, and greenery. Everything gone! Ugly, gaping holes left big spaces in the beadboard. The despicable rodent headed for the chandelier, "No!" I screamed inwardly, "you can't eat the light." Yet I watched and heard it gnaw and crunch until the beautiful fixture disappeared light bulbs and all. I looked around; the rooms were bare and unsightly. Not even linoleum covered the floor. It was uglier than any house I had ever seen. The rat had literally eaten us out of house and home. I woke up in a sweat.

"What did that mean?" I questioned God. I knew that many times God allows us to see in a dream Satan's plans for our future. That way we can bind it from happening like Jesus said,

Whatsoever thou shalt bind on earth shall be bound in heaven and whatsoever thou shalt loose on earth shall be loosed in heaven (Matthew 16:19 and 18:18). I figured if I pray to bind a thing on earth, God hears and binds it in the heavenlies where Satan and his demons dwell. When God binds them they can't touch me. I also knew that Matthew 12:29 says *How can one enter into a strong man's house and spoil his goods except he first bind the strong man and then he will spoil his house.* Well, someone had spoiled my house and I was ready for a fight. First, I needed to bind him so I could spoil his activity and take back my stuff.

"What does the rat represent in the dream?" I wondered and began to analyze it. I knew it was spiritual. He ate the bed - that meant our rest. He consumed the couch and chairs which was our relaxation. The desk was next which represented study. Then the rat devoured the dining table. What rat is eating our spiritual food? I wondered. It crunched up the dining chairs. That was a symbol of the fellowship around the table. Then it nibbled all the decorations off of the walls which represented the beauty in our life. And finally the rodent gobbled up the light. I knew the Bible tells us that Jesus is the light of the world. Without Him we sit in darkness.

What has invaded my home and devoured all these things? Suddenly, it hit me. The rotten rodent crawled out from under the television. That was it. Time spent watching television was robbing us of time for other things, important things like:

Reading and studying the Bible - the desk was gone,

Spiritual food, daily devotions, church attendance and talking around the table with our family - the dining table and chairs were devoured.

Relaxing with friends - the sofa and lounge chairs were missing.

Rest and sleep was affected - the bed was no longer there.

The blessings of God were dissipating - the wall

decorations were eaten up.

Was Jesus the light vanishing too? The chandelier no longer hung over my life.

I knew if I continued allowing the television rat to steal my time, all the beauty in my life would disappear. The only thing left at the end of life would be an empty, ugly decaying shell with little accomplished for God.

"Help me, Lord," I cried. "Help me to get that rat out of my life. Help me to turn off the television."

Am I the only one entertaining this spiritual rodent? I don't think so, but your rat may be something else. It could be sports, parties, movies, hobby, excessive work, ambition, making money, or just plain being lazy. Examine your life and see what steals your time and energy that you could put to good use for God and your family.

FIFTH PIECE OF ARMOR

HELMET OF SALVATION

Take the helmet of salvation

We all know that a helmet covers and protects our head, the thinking part of the body - the decision maker. Our whole body is controlled by the brain inside the head. If a person is hit in the head it can cause damage to the rest of their body. Through a blow to the head one may be paralyzed so that the legs do not move and walking is impossible. Or the brain damage may cause the person to think incorrectly. The individual may be unable to care for herself, unable to live a normal life. Through a head injury, eyes may be blinded, speech affected and hearing lost. I'd say protecting the brain is the most valuable step you can take.

When David hit the giant, Goliath, in the head with a rock it knocked him down and David cut off his head. Goliath lost his life because of an injury to the head.

Satan also knows the importance of the brain. He knows the way to defeat us is to start with our brain - our thinking. Thoughts are as important as spoken words. Thoughts and words have creative power. *As a man thinketh in his heart so is he (Proverbs 23:7)*. The Hebrew word in this text for *think* means to split or open, to act as a gatekeeper, to think. Our thoughts open or close the gate to our lives and to eternal life.

Love thinketh no evil (I Corinthians 13:5).

SALVATION

Put on the helmet of salvation. The word *salvation,* as used here, means defense. We must put on the helmet of defense to protect our thinking. How do we do that? The Bible says that we should *think on things that are true, honest, just, pure, lovely, of a good report; virtuous, and praise worthy (Philippians 4:8).*

Let's dissect this list to see what we can learn concerning the things we are to think about. Whatsoever things are:

TRUE

How many times do we think about lies someone told us about another person. It makes us feel bad towards them. We mull it over and over in our minds until we are nearly sick wondering if it's true. Forget the lies. Think about a truth that you know about that person, a good quality in them. Pray for God to help them overcome the bad ones.

HONEST

Don't dwell on dishonest issues. If in doubt, leave it out. Think about truth. Jesus is the truth. Think about him and the truth of the Bible.

JUST

Do you listen to accounts of injustice, stories about people who have been unfair to others or judges who make wrong decisions? You think about it until you are angry. Instead, remember the good things

159

people do. Rejoice in justice.

PURE

How many times do we hear unholy reports about affairs? We watch TV and see impure acts that are a big part of most movies and TV programs today. We dwell on them and taint our morals.

Years before my dream about the huge rat that ate the interior of my house, I was hooked on a couple of soap operas. That's all, only two. I mean, I didn't sit around all afternoon watching them or anything like that. I still did my work and put food on the table at the right time.

I told my experience earlier in the book of the jealous spirit that tormented me as a result of opening that door. It may not be wrong for others to watch soap operas. A wonderful lady in our church watched them every day and they didn't affect her. She was a widow and she said it was like having company come to see her. She was one of the, happiest people I have ever known.

Each person has to figure out what they can and cannot do. The Bible says to work out your own salvation with fear and trembling.

One reason that I couldn't watch them is that my favorite soap came on when we ate our evening meal. I was so engrossed that I didn't want anyone to say a word because I might miss something. My two oldest children were young and I didn't want them to even say, "Please pass the bread."

The second reason was that by feeding my mind

160

impure material, it malfunctioned and I began acting strange. I told my husband that women were eyeing him, trying to entice him, and accused him of enjoying this imaginary flirtation.

Men don't like to be accused of things, especially when they are not guilty. You can imagine the strife my words instigated in our home. I cannot tell you how miserable I felt. Overwhelmed, I cried out to God to show me what was wrong with me that caused these bad thoughts and created strife in my home. Desperate for help, I had to have an answer soon and asked Him to show me that night.

After prayer, I crawled into bed. The television sat at the foot of our bed and as I drifted off to sleep I heard it click. It startled me as all of the family members were in bed. Wondering who turned on the television I raised up, looked at the screen, and expected to see a picture. The screen remained dark. In my spirit I heard a voice say, "That's your problem. The soap operas are affecting your thinking."

I fell back on the bed disappointed. "God," I said, "I love those soap operas. I can't give them up. I don't think I have what it takes to stop watching them." Then I said, "If You will take away the desire I will give them up, but You have to do it. I can't do it by myself." I really didn't believe He would. The next morning when I awoke, to my surprise, I had no desire to ever see another soap opera as long as I lived. God set me free.

Before long, God delivered me from the jealous spirit that overtook me as a result of feeding my mind on impure material. I closed the door on soap operas that allowed Satan into my mind and stuck the helmet of salvation firmly back on my head to protect and defend my thoughts.

SCRIPTURES CONCERNING THE MIND

Be not conformed to this world: but be ye transformed by the renewing of your mind, that ye may prove what is that good, and acceptable, and perfect, will of God (Romans 12:2).

That he might sanctify and cleanse it with the washing of water by the word (Ephesians 5:26). If our mind is polluted, the Bible will cleanse it.

Not by works of righteousness which we have done, but according to his mercy he saved us, by the washing of regeneration, and renewing of the Holy Ghost; which he shed on us abundantly through Jesus Christ our Savior (Titus 3:5-6). This Scripture promises that the Holy Ghost will renew us.

Is your mind polluted? Put the word of God in it by reading and memorizing scripture and the Holy Spirit will wash and renew it.

I think of the mind as a video tape. Everything you have heard or seen is recorded on it. That's why what we see on television, movies, computer, or read in books and magazines, is so important. These pictures and words are permanently taped to our mind as thoughts. Satan likes to rewind and continually replay them. The Bible and the Holy Spirit are the only things that can erase the tape.

162

Let's continue with our word study. The next word on the list is:

LOVELY

Do you think about things that are lovely or ugly? Sin is ugly. Don't think about it any longer than you have to when you pray for the one committing it. Lovely things are home, family, flowers, butterflies, birds, bunnies, sunshine, meadows, waterfalls, oceans and of course heaven. Most of all, Jesus is altogether lovely. Think about Him.

GOOD REPORT

The evening news is not a good report. If it bears on your mind, don't watch it. You'll live without hashing over all the sin and evil that is going on in the world. Smith Wigglesworth, a mighty man of God who saw the sick healed and the dead raised to life, would not allow a newspaper in his house. He did not want a bad report or negative idea in his home. Television was not invented back then but I am sure he would not have allowed it near his home. A wise and godly man I'd say.

I know a woman who is establishing a business. She told me recently that she couldn't afford cable since her money has to go into her business, so she gave away her television. Since then life has changed dramatically. She and her husband actually sit in the living room and talk. They are closer than ever. Together they read and study to acquire the education they lack. Both have become Christians and are enjoying life to the fullest. After all didn't Jesus say that He, not television, came to give us life and that more abundantly?

VIRTUOUS

Virtue means moral goodness, chastity, prudence, temperance, fortitude, faith, hope, and charity. This gives you a good idea of many virtuous things to fix your mind upon.

PRAISE WORTHY

Praise is to: express approbation or admiration of, commend, glorify. How often are our thoughts on admirable things others have done? Do we think and speak of these things instead of cutting people down for bad things they do? Are we commending each other even in our thoughts, or are we envious of their good gifts.

We need to think of good things; leave out the negative. Trap the rat of 'stinking thinking' and replace it with 'lean, clean thoughts' by putting on the helmet of salvation.

HOW DO I PUT ON THE HELMET OF SALVATION?

First, if you have not accepted Jesus, the author of salvation, accept Him now. Pray the prayer of forgiveness suggested in the first chapter of this book then:

1. **Put right things in your mind.**

Be careful what you see, hear, and read. This includes TV, videos, DVDs, movies, computer, books, magazines, etc.

2. **Read the Bible and good Christian books**. Watch only wholesome movies and limit time spent in front of the television and on the internet.

3. **Practice being thankful**. Think of all the things for which you are thankful. Write a list, post it on your bathroom mirror and read it each time you brush your teeth.

If you do all the above Rafferty the Rat or Rosie the Rodent will not have a chance to distract you, devour your time or foul your thoughts. Your mind will dwell on good things and create a wonderful life.

No rats in your thoughts.

OUR ONLY

WEAPON

Sword of the Spirit

We have talked about the armor of God which is for our protection. The armor does nothing to the enemy. It is strictly for our benefit. It covers us so that we gain protection from the enemy's attacks.

Now let's talk about how to do damage to the enemy. Can I foul his strategy? What kind of pesticide do I use? I want to cut him down to size. Better yet, let's freeze him in his tracks!

Though we walk in the flesh we do not war after the flesh. For the weapons of our warfare are not carnal, but mighty through God to the pulling down of strong holds. Casting down imaginations, and every high thing that exalteth itself against the knowledge of God, and bringing into captivity every thought to the obedience of Christ (II Corinthians 10:3-5).

This Scripture describes what our weapon is not and what our weapon will do. Let's look at our original text for this chapter to find our weapon. This section of the Scripture tells us that our weapon is *the sword of the spirit which is the word of God.*

John describes Jesus in Revelation 19:14-15 and

also in Revelation 1:16. In these verses, Jesus has a sharp sword coming out of His mouth. With this sword He smites and destroys the enemy. In other words what comes out of Jesus mouth defeats Satan. It is the only pesticide that He needs. It is the same with you and me. What comes out of our mouth defeats the enemy - Satan? It is our only weapon but it manifests in several different forms. Let's examine them.

EIGHT WAYS TO USE THE TWO EDGED SWORD AGAINST SATAN, OUR ENEMY

1. QUOTE THE WORD OF GOD - This means the Bible. Jesus quoted Scripture during each temptation in the wilderness and Satan was defeated each time.

In Jesus' day, only boys attended school. Girls were not allowed. The boy's textbook was the first five books of the Old Testament which they had to memorize. Think about it! We have trouble memorizing a few verses. Jesus could have been familiar with the Scriptures from learning them in school or He could have known them because He was the Son of God. Either way, He knew them and He quoted them often.

We need to do the same.

Tempted in the wilderness after His baptism, Jesus' weapon against Satan was Scripture. The story is recorded in Luke chapter four. Jesus fasted forty days and afterward became hungry. The devil appealed to His fleshly desire for food. He said "Command the stones to be made bread." He knew that Jesus helped create the universe and possessed the power to do this small task.

168

Jesus stopped Satan in his tracks when He sprayed the powerful 'insecticide' of the Word of God. He quoted Deuteronomy 8:3, *Man shall not live by bread alone, but by every word of God.* Satan squirmed as the fumes settled in his lungs. He lost that round, defeated by Scripture.

In the second temptation, Satan took Jesus to a high mountain and in an instant showed Him all the kingdoms of the world. He said, "I will give you all their authority and splendor, for it has been given to me and I can give it to anyone. So if You worship me, it will all be Yours."

Jesus quoted Deuteronomy 6:13 and 10:20 *Thou shalt worship the Lord thy God, and him only shalt thou serve.* Again Satan cringed as the sting of the Word hit him. Jesus won another round with Scripture.

The third temptation was a test to see if Jesus really believed He was the Son of God. Satan took Him to a high pinnacle of the temple and said "If you are the Son of God cast Yourself down from here." Then Satan used Jesus' tactic of quoting Scripture. He recited, *It is written, He shall give His angels charge over thee, to keep thee: And in their hands they shall bear thee up, lest at any time thou dash thy foot against a stone (Psalm 91:11).*

You see, Satan knows the Word too, but he takes it out of context and uses it in the wrong manner. He will try to do that to you He will twist the Scripture and make it sound like something that is not true. But Jesus was not confused by Satan's misuse of the verse. He answered with more of the Word, *Thou shalt not tempt the Lord thy God (Deuteronomy 6:16).*

We should not tempt God by doing things that we know will hurt us and then expect Him to prevent death or injury. Jesus did not have to prove to Satan that He was the Son of God. The Lord knew who He was without doing something stupid like jumping off a building.

Satan still tries to utilize the three temptations. He wants us to use the authority we have as a believer to create something for our own advantage.

He still tries to win our allegiance. He promises wealth, fame and fun if we will worship him.

He attempts to push us into doing stupid things to prove that we belong to God. He puts doubt into our mind and we begin to wonder if we really are a Christian. Don't believe him or fall for his tricks. Remember that the Bible says, h*e is a liar and the father of it (John 8:44).*

Satan also uses people to talk to you. Don't let people talk you into doing something wrong to prove a point. Young guys will tell a girl, "If you really love me, you will have sex with me." WRONG. If he really loves you, he will not ask for sex until after you are married. Though it sounds old-fashioned it is still God's plan and is for your safety. You don't need an illegitimate child or the guilt of an abortion or a disease from a man that may have had sex with many women before you.

Jesus won the final round with Satan by again fogging him with the Word of God. Satan bit the dust and left Him alone for a season. Unfortunately, he planned to make a comeback. He does us the same way. When we defeat him with the Word of God he leaves for a while, but he'll be back.

Get your Scripture ready for the next fight.

2. THE SPOKEN WORD

Don't disregard words spoken by the Holy Ghost. Tongues and interpretation, prophecy, words of wisdom, and words of knowledge are all part of the sword of the spirit which is the Word of God. All of these can put the enemy to flight.

TODAY THE HOLY GHOST STILL SPEAKS

A WORD FROM GOD

The Holy Ghost moved on holy men of old to write the Bible. The same Spirit moves on holy men today to speak as He gives the utterance. When someone today speaks with tongues and interpretation, prophecy, gives a word of knowledge or a word of wisdom, we judge whether or not it is of God by the Bible - the written word. If it does not measure up to the Bible, we disregard it.

Paul said if an angel from heaven comes and gives you a gospel other than the one he preached, the one we have in the Bible, let it be accursed. However, if it does measure up, why would we want to throw it out? We accept it as a spoken word from God. It strengthens us adding fuel in our fight against Satan.

3. PRAYER

Nothing happens in the spirit world until we pray. When we pray, Satan takes a terrible beating. My mother and father were saved because of prayer. Their mailman prayed for God to save someone on that block of his mail route. It was my parents. God dealt with Mama at home and Daddy while on the job. Both were convicted on the same day because the mailman prayed.

Who prayed for your salvation? Somebody did or you wouldn't be saved. For whom are you praying? Will someone be saved because you prayed? Prayer is a powerful sword to defeat Satan in other people's lives as well as our own.

FIVE TYPES OF PRAYER.

A. Supplication

The Greek definition in the New Testament for *supplication* is prayer, request.

In the Old Testament the Hebrew word means - To be rubbed or worn, to stroke (in flattering). Entreat beseech, woman in travail. Graciousness - entreaty, favor, grace, to bend or stoop in kindness to an inferior. To favor, bestow, merciful, show mercy, have pity upon. Move to favor by petition. To intercede, pray: -entreat, judge, make supplication.

In English, *supplication* means to kneel down, pray, to fold, double up, to ask for humbly and earnestly as by prayer.

Are we kneeling down to humbly ask God to have pity upon the lost, to show mercy and save them? Are we beseeching Him to favor and bless our friends and enemies? We should. Jesus taught us to do this in His sermon on the mount. I am glad the mailman prayed for my parents to be saved or I may never have found Jesus.

On the day of Pentecost, one hundred and twenty people stayed in the upper room as Jesus had commanded them. They expected the Holy Spirit. While they waited the Bible says:

These all continued with one accord in prayer and ***supplication*** *(Acts 1:14).*

They were praying for the promise. When the Holy Spirit came, they were all affected and so was the entire city. Three thousand souls were added to the kingdom of God that day.

Think what would happen in our city if we banded together to pray. The church in Seoul, Korea did. They went to a mountain every Friday and prayed all night. So many souls were saved that it became the largest church in the world.

Paul said, *Praying always with all prayer and* ***supplication*** *in the Spirit, and watching thereunto with all perseverance and* ***supplication*** *for all saints (Ephesians 6:18).* We need to pray for the lost but also for all saints. By praying we can help each other defeat the enemy in our lives.

Philippians 4:6 says to let our requests be known to God by prayer and ***supplication*** with thanksgiving. Let's not forget to thank God for answered prayers when we make our requests.

173

B. Intercession:

Intercede means to plead with a person for another.

*I exhort therefore, that first of all supplications, prayers, **intercessions**, and giving of thanks, be made for all men (I Timothy 2:1).* We are exhorted to intercede for people around us so that Satan is defeated in their life. We must be concerned enough to take time to plead for others. It is easy to intercede for a family member because their problems affect us. Could we be that concerned as this Scripture says and pray for all men?

The law of reciprocity works in this area of our lives. What we do for others will return. If we intercede for others someone will pray for us.

C. Asking

Jesus said, *Ask and ye shall receive (Matthew 7:7).* Case closed. It's that simple.

The word for ask actually means to continue asking. Don't give up because you have not received yet. The Bible is true. Jesus said that you will get what you ask for. Be sure it is what God wants for you before you ask.

D. Binding and Loosing

How can one enter into a strong man's house, and spoil his goods, except he first bind the strong man? And then he will spoil his house (Matthew 12:29).

The Pharisees accused Jesus of casting out devils by Beelzebub the prince of devils. Jesus explained that this would be a divided kingdom. It would be Satan working

174

against Satan. He said if you are going to spoil a house Satan controls you must first bind Satan. Then you can ruin his house.

And I will give unto thee the keys of the kingdom of heaven: and whatsoever thou shalt bind on earth shall be bound in heaven; and whatsoever thou shalt loose on earth shall be loosed in heaven (Matthew 16:19).

How much power over the bugs in our life do we have through this statement of Jesus? If we only could grasp the magnitude of it, nothing would stop us from serving Jesus to the fullest extent.

E. Agreement

If two of you shall agree on earth as touching anything that they shall ask, it shall be done for them of my Father which is in heaven. For where two or three are gathered together in my name, there am I in the midst of them (Matthew 19:19).

Have you prayed the prayer of agreement with a friend? It often brings quick results. Try it. Give Satan a black eye. Why do you think he causes so much strife and disagreements? He knows the power in our agreement.

I have noticed when my husband and I agree in prayer, we always get an answer.

I have pointed out five ways of praying. Each one is powerful against Satan if only we will do them.

4. PLEAD THE BLOOD OF JESUS

As a child I remember my mother saying "I plead

the blood of Jesus over this situation." I thought that statement sounded a little crazy. Later in life when I had a son on drugs, a man on television said, "If you are praying over a lost loved one you need to plead the blood of Jesus over him every day. When you wake up every morning say, 'Lord, I plead the blood of Jesus over my son's (put your son or daughter's name there) mind, soul, body, and spirit this day and night. I thank you for his salvation. Dress him in the full armor of God. I thank you for it. In Jesus' name I pray. Amen.'"

I began to do that and immediately noticed a difference in my own attitude. I felt a release in my spirit. Worry seemed to roll off of me. What a relief from a situation out of my control. God could now work in my son's life.

That was not the only type of prayer I prayed for him but it was one that brought me peace and defeated the devil of worry.

5. COMMAND SATAN

I read of a man who prayed for a wayward daughter. God revealed a petition that released his daughter from a life of drugs. He simply cried out, "Satan, I command you to desist in your maneuvers against my daughter in Jesus' name." He felt a great sense of victory. Before long, the daughter was home, saved from her sins and drug free. Yes, we have the right to command Satan to take his hands off of our loved ones. Let's use our authority. Satan has no business butting into our family's life unless we give him the green light.

Jesus commanded Satan to leave people. *When the even was come, they brought unto him many that were possessed with devils; and he cast out the spirits with his word, and healed all that were sick (Matthew 6:16).*

6. POSITIVE WORDS

Negative words are of Satan. Positive words come from God. Negative words allow Satan to work in our lives. Positive words allow God to work. Our angels cannot help us when we talk negative. We stop the flow of God. Negative words re-enforce evil, create fear, worry, anger, strife, confusion, feuds, loss, divorce and even death.

Positive words create joy, strength, health, friendship, love, peace, understanding, knowledge, and life.

The Psalmist asks the question, *Do you want a long, good life?* The next verse tells us how to have one. It says, *Keep your tongue from evil and your lips from speaking guile (Ps 34:12-13).*

When I first read this I said, "I already do that. I don't curse or talk bad." Then I looked up the word EVIL in Hebrew. I was shocked at the depth of its meaning. It means: adversity, affliction, bad, calamity, displeasure, distress, evil, (man, thing), grief, harm, hurt, mischief, misery, sad, sorry, trouble, wrong.

All of these are negative things that I am not supposed to talk about if I want a good life.

But don't we like to talk about all of these things - the calamities we hear about on the news and our afflictions and grief, the things that hurt us and displease us, other

177

peoples mischief and misery? These subjects make up a good portion of our conversations.

The word GOOD in this Scripture means: beautiful, best, better, bountiful, cheerful, at ease, fair, favor, fine, glad, good, joyful, kindly, kindness, graciously, liketh, loving, merry, pleasant, please, pleasure, precious, prosperity, ready, sweet, wealth, welfare, well.

Wow! Those are the things God's Word says makes up the good life we can have if we keep our lips from speaking EVIL and guile. GUILE means: in the sense of deceiving, fraud, deceit, false, feigned, guile, subtle, treachery.

Need I say more? To defeat the devil and have a good life, don't lie or deceive in any way. Don't talk about all the bad in life, but look for the good and talk about theat. Jesus is the best so let's talk about Him and live the good life.

7. PRAISE

A perfect example of how praise defeats the enemy is found in the Old Testament when Jehoshaphat, king of Judah, faced a problem. The soldiers of Moab and Ammon, with others, came to war against Judah.

Jehoshaphat stood in the Temple and cried out to God telling Him . . . *If when evil cometh upon us . . . we stand before this house, and in thy presence, (for thy name is in this house,) and cry unto thee in our affliction, then thou will hear and help (II Chronicles 20:9).*

That was not the end. A prophet told Jehoshaphat,

Be not afraid nor dismayed by reason of this great multitude; for the battle is not yours, but God's. (II Chronicles 20:16). On hearing this, the Levites praised God with a loud voice.

The next morning Jehoshaphat said to the people, "Believe the Lord your God, so shall ye be established; believe his prophets, so shall ye prosper" (II Chronicles 20:20).

He sent singers and those who praised the Lord to battle first. All they did was sing and praise God while the enemy killed each other. They won the war without fighting. There was so much loot of riches and precious jewels that it took three days to gather. What a victory!

Many times, I have entered the church where my husband was pastor, stood alone in the sanctuary, and prayed Jehoshaphat's prayer. Then while walking up and down the aisle I have praised God to the top of my voice. Sometimes singing in the Spirit other times shouting out praises. I always hoped no one with a key unlocked the door, came in, saw me and heard me. They might have thought I was crazy, but God heard and defeated the enemy without any other help from me. All He wanted was my loud praise.

Yes, the Psalmist did say to praise Him with a loud voice. I know God's not deaf, but he's not nervous, either. He loves our loud praise and Satan hates it because it causes his defeat.

8. PRAY AND SING IN TONGUES

Our greatest answers to prayer come when we offer the perfect prayer, one the Holy Ghost prays through us. *Likewise the Spirit also helpeth our infirmities; for we know not what we should pray for as we ought; but the Spirit itself maketh intercession for us with groanings which cannot be uttered. And he that searcheth the hearts knoweth what is the mind of the Spirit, because he maketh intercession for the saints according to the will of God (Romans 8:26-27).*

In Isaiah 59:16 God wondered that there was no intercessor; no one to pray for the people. Then Jesus came, gave His life on a cross and now the New Testament tells us - *He ever liveth to make intercession for them (Hebrews 7:25).*

He said God would send the Holy Spirit. He sent him on the day of Pentecost. The Spirit is the intercessor. When we allow him to pray through us to intercede He always defeats Satan.

THE STANDARD

In Bible days, a STANDARD was similar to our flag. It displayed an ensign or emblem. When the troops went to war, they carried their standard with each tribe's individual ensign to their camp site and hung it above their tents to identify where each unit camped.

The word standard actually means to flit, chase, impel, deliver, escape, make to flee, put to flight. So when a fierce, winning tribe displayed their standard with their ensign painted on, it scared the enemy and caused them to run.

Isaiah 11:10 says, *And in that day there shall be a root of Jesse, which shall stand for an ensign of the people.* We know that Jesus was the root of Jesse. Verse 12 of the same chapter says, *He shall 'set up' for an ensign for the nations.*

I wondered - *how does He 'set up' for an ensign for the nations?* Then I saw it clearly. Soldiers lifted up Jesus on the cross and dropped it into a hole to make it stand. 'Set up' on that hill, the old rugged cross became the standard for all who believe in the power of the blood of Jesus.

And he (the devil, our enemy) *shall pass over to his stronghold for fear, and his princes shall be afraid of the ensign (Isaiah 31:9).*

Ensign means to strike, beat, give wounds, cast forth, clap, kill, slaughter, slay, smite, give stripes, wound.

Who was beaten with many stripes, wounded and killed for our salvation? JESUS. He is our ensign on our standard - the cross. This Scripture tells me that the devil is afraid of this ensign and standard - Jesus on the cross.

This is the mental picture I received that day. *When the enemy (Satan) comes against you like a flood, the spirit of the Lord shall lift up a standard against him (Isaiah 59:19).*

I could see God's children being beaten by Satan. They were bowled over, taking the lashes and praying all the while.

Suddenly, when it seemed the war would never end, they remembered. With a bold thrust they held up the cross of Calvary in the devil's face. It reminded him that God has already lifted up a standard against him when Jesus was lifted up on that cross for our salvation.

With a shriek Satan drops his whip, shields his eyes, and runs away as fast as he can, moaning all the way.

The next time Satan bothers you, HOLD UP THE CROSS our standard that bears our ensign – JESUS.

When you remind him what Jesus did for you there, Satan and his demons will flee.

PART IV

WINNING

END OF THE WAR

OUT COME OF THE BATTLE

The devil that deceived them was cast into the lake of fire and brimstone . . . and shall be tormented day and night forever and ever.

(Rev. 20:10)

All of our life we fight against evil forces. Day after day we put on the armor of God and stand against the wiles or trickery of the devil. We war against his demons - evil spirits who try to overcome us or distract us so that we lose sight of the eternal goal. We wield the sword of the Spirit making big gashes in the enemy.

When he retaliates, we pick up the shield of Faith to stop his hateful darts. We don shoes of Peace and get along with family, neighbors, and yes, even fellow church members who are less than perfect. There is a purpose in it, we know, but sometimes the vision is cloudy. We wonder if the battle will ever end and if it is worth all the effort and sacrifice.

Jesus promises in the book of Revelation certain rewards for those who overcome the evil one. To see these promised blessings, let's look at Him as He walks among the candlesticks that represent the churches in Asia.

He wears a long white robe with a golden band around His chest. His head and His hair are white as snow. His eyes are like a flame of fire. His feet are like polished

184

brass glowing in a furnace. His voice is like the sound of many waters. He holds seven stars in His right hand, which represent the angels or pastors of the seven churches of Asia. His face shines like the sun at its full strength. A sharp two-edged sword comes out of His mouth.

His awesome appearance causes John to faint. Jesus picks him up and says, *Don't be afraid. I am the First and the Last. I am the Living One. I died, but see! I am alive again for evermore. And I have the keys of death and hell.*

REWARDS

Jesus then describes the deeds and rewards of the seven churches of Asia. See if you find yourself in one of these.

EPHESUS

Jesus describes Himself to the church at Ephesus as the one who holds the seven stars and walks among the candlesticks. The seven stars, one for each church, are believed to be either the angels or pastors of the churches. The Greek word for stars, has to do with skin and positioning. This makes me believe He holds His pastors in His hand and attends the services of His churches. Pastor, lift up your head. Jesus knows everything you go through.

Jesus *commended* the church at *Ephesus* for six qualities: 1. Hard work. 2. Patience, 3. They double check the claims of those who profess to be apostles of Christ, discovering them to be liars. 4. They suffer for Christ's sake without quitting. 5. They refuse to tolerate sin among the members. 6. They hate the sins of the Nicolaitans* who practice prostitution at the temple of Diana, (one of the wonders of the world), believe in the community of wives, and teach that fornication and adultery are not sinful. *Dake

God says He hates this doctrine.

Jesus *admonishes* Ephesus for one glaring fault - they lost their first love and now work out of duty. He warns them to get back to their first love and to work the way they did before they lost it. He says if they don't repent, He will remove their candlestick – their church.

One wonders if they returned to their first love or if God removed their candlestick because the site of Ephesus is now covered with ruins, the residence of a miserable Turkish village without one Christian in it.

THE BLESSING FOR OBEDIENCE

He promises those who overcome: they shall eat of the tree of life in the paradise of God. Think of it, to live forever with God with no more hunger.

SMYRNA

Jesus describes Himself to the church at Smyrna as the first and the last who was dead and now is alive.

Smyrna is a rich city, but Christians there live in poverty. God says they are rich spiritually yet they suffer persecution for the Lord. Their enemies slander them. Some are thrown into prison for the cause of Christ. Hypocrites in the church blaspheme by falsely saying they are Jews, but are actually from the synagogue of Satan.

THE BLESSINGS for remaining faithful to Christ in spite of persecution and imprisonment are:

A crown of Life.

Never to be hurt by the second death.

The first death is the separation of the soul from the body. We call it dying. The second death is when the soul is separated from God and cast into hell.

I prefer to remain faithful, receive the crown of life, and avoid the second death. How about you?

PERGAMOS

Jesus describes Himself to the pastor at Pergamos, as He who has the sharp two-edged sword, equipped to cut out the false doctrines of this church.

Pergamos is believed to be where the ancient Babylonian cult was moved from Babylon. Jesus calls it the seat of Satan and says that Satan dwells there.

In spite of the wickedness around them, God sees the works of the Christians at Pergamos. He sees that they hold fast His name and have not denied His faith even when the church leader, Antipas, is put to death in a burning brazen bull.*Dake

God has a few things against the church at *Pergamos.* Some of the members hold the doctrine of Balaam which teaches that if Balak gives his most beautiful women to the men of Israel to commit idolatry and adultery, and to eat food offered to idols, God will curse Israel. They love the wages of unrighteousness.

Others in the church hold to the doctrine of the Nicolaitans, which includes all types of sexual perversion. The doctrine God hates

GOD SAYS - REPENT

THE REWARD for those who repent:

God promises them food - hidden manna.

God will give them a white stone with a new name written in it that no one knows except the one who receives.

In Bible days, when you went to court and the verdict was settled, you were *guilty and condemned if you received a black stone. A white stone meant that you were pardoned. Conquerors in the public games were also given a white stone with their name in it which entitled them to support for the rest of their lives at public expense. These stones were known as victory stones. *Dake

I love this reward! All of my life I have hated having a boy's name. God says if I repent I can have a new name in a white stone with His support throughout eternity. I'll never want or be without. He will give me hidden manna. We know that is food but the kind of food is hidden until we arrive in Heaven.

Praise God! He has so many surprises waiting for us, the over-comers.

THYATIRA

To the church in Thyatira Jesus describes Himself as the Son of God who has eyes like a flame of fire and feet

188

like fine brass. I believe His eyes burn with anger because of the sin in this church.

God commends the church at Thyatira for their works, charity, service, faith, patience, and increased works. They start out working and increase their works so the last are greater than the first.

He says He has a few things against them. They allow a woman named Jezebel to teach filthy doctrine, seducing God's people to commit fornication and to eat food sacrificed to idols. God gives her a time to repent of her sex sins, but she refuses. He says she and all who follow her, unless they repent, will suffer in a bed of affliction and her children will die. Fornication causes disease. Sin kills.

Jesus speaks to the people in the church who had not sinned. Those who had not learned Satan's so-called deep secrets. He encourages them to hold fast to their faith and continue their works.

PROMISED BLESSINGS for keeping His works until the end or remaining in the war:

He promised power over the nations to rule with a rod of iron and crush all resistance.

He also promised the morning star - which is Jesus.

SARDIS

To the church at Sardis, Jesus describes Himself as having the seven Spirits of God and the seven stars. What does He mean by seven spirits of God? Revelation 5:6 says

189

He has seven horns and seven eyes, which are the seven Spirits of God.

We know there is only one Holy Spirit. The number seven represents completion or fullness. When God finished creating the earth and all that is in it, He rested on the seventh day. He was finished; His work completed. Seven means the complete Holy Spirit or fullness of the Holy Spirit. Jesus is the first to have the Holy Spirit without measure (John 3:34). The Bible speaks of different measures of the Spirit.

*1. Mosaic portion (Numbers 11:17).

2. Mosaic portion divided into 71 portions (Numbers 11:16-17).

3. Elijah portion (II Kings 2:9).

4. Double portion (II Kings 2:9-10).

5. Elijah portion on John the Baptist (Luke 1:15-17).

6. Earnest of the Spirit (II Corinthians 1:22; 5:5;

I John 4:13; Philippians 1:19).

7. The Spirit without measure (John 3:34; Isaiah 11:2; 42:1; 61:1; Luke 4:16-21; Acts 10:38).

8. Spirit baptism or baptismal measure (Matthew. 3:11;20:22-23; Luke 3:16; John 1:31-34; Acts 1:4-8; 3:1-21; 8:15-24; 10:44-48; 11:14-18; 15:7-11; 19:1-7; Galatians 3:14).

9. The fullness of God (Ephesians 3:19; Ro.. 15:29).

10. Rivers of living water (John 7:37-39).

11. Full anointing of the Spirit and endued with power from on high (Luke 24:49; John 14:12-15). *

* Dake

God says to the church at Sardis that He knows their works and their name that they are alive, but really they are dead. He tells them that other things are about to die and they should strengthen those things to keep them alive.

He says they are not perfect before God. They should remember the first time they heard about the gospel and how they received it readily. "Don't let it slip out of your hands," He warns, "but hold fast and repent." He cautions that He will come and they will not be ready if they don't heed this warning.

He commends them that a few people in Sardis are pure, and have not defiled their garment.

THE REWARD OF THE FAITHFUL

"They will walk with Me in white for they are worthy," Jesus said. He adds that all who overcomes will be clothed in white raiment.

He will not blot out their names from the Book of Life, but will confess their name before His Father and his Father's angels.

Contrary to some teaching, this scripture sounds like our name could be blotted out of the book of life and we could lose our salvation.

PHILADELPHIA

Jesus describes Himself to the church in Philadelphia as the one who is holy, true, has the key (power and authority) of David.

Concerning them He says: "I know your works, you have a little strength, you have kept my word and you have not denied my name. I have set before you an open door and no man can shut it." Is that the door of opportunity? Let's walk through when we see it open.

God promises to expose liars in the church at Philadelphia and humble the liars before them. He promises to keep them from the hour of temptation that will come on the entire world.

He warns them to hold fast what they have, and don't let anyone take their crown. If I refuse to obey God's call on my life it sounds like He will call someone else to do my job and they will get my crown.

REWARD FOR THE OVERCOMERS

To those who overcome He promises to make them a pillar in the temple of God. A pillar stands for stability and authority. It's not going anyplace, but will be there forever.

Jesus promises to write three names on us: The name of God, the name of the city of God and His new name.

LAODICEA

Jesus describes Himself to the church of Laodicea

as the Amen, the faithful and true witness, the beginning of the creation of God.

He says to them that they are neither cold nor hot. He wishes they were one or the other. He is nauseated with their lukewarm condition and says He will spew them out of His mouth

Though they boast to be rich with plenty of goods and have need of nothing, they are unaware that they are actually wretched and miserable and poor and blind and naked.

About being poor, He says, "Buy of Me gold that is tried in the fire." In other words, I have the real deal. My gold is purified. When you have it, you are rich.

He says, "Buy white raiment from Me so you won't be ashamed of your nakedness." He will cloth us with white raiment of purity, but it will cost us . . . our own desires and plans - for His.

He says, "Anoint your eyes with eye-salve that you may see." He doesn't want us deceived. Jesus warned many times in the Gospels against being deceived. Open your eyes to the truth as God reveals it to you.

He concludes with the fact that He chastens the ones he loves, and warns them to repent.

He gives an invitation to open the door to Him. He stands and knocks and wants to come in and dine.

If you repent, let Him come in, and overcome evil, He promises that you can sit with Him in His throne even as He overcame and sat down with His Father on His throne.

We have seen the promised rewards for the seven churches of Asia of those who overcome. Let's look at other promises God makes to believers.

He says He will wipe away all tears from our eyes.

He says He is going to prepare us a place.

He says He will come for us.

Let's imagine the end of the battle. We stop fighting Satan. Jesus wins the final battle with His words - the sword of His mouth. One angel will bind Satan and throw him into the pit.

We will never again be sick or sad or lonely, never be afraid or do without. Never will anyone put us down or hurt us. No more problems or anxiety, but peace and joy will reign.

It will certainly be worth anything we go through in this life to reap the benefits when we stand before God at the end of the battle.

Having done all to stand, WE WILL STAND.

WE ARE OVERCOMERS!

SOLDIER'S PLEDGE- ARMY OF GOD

(Author Unknown)

I am a soldier in the army of the Lord.

Jesus Christ is my Commanding Officer.

The Holy Bible is my code of conduct.

Faith, Prayer and God's Word are my

Weapons of warfare,

I have been taught by the Holy Spirit, trained

By experience, tried by adversity and tested by fire.

I am a volunteer in the army, and I am enlisted

For eternity.

I will either retire in this army at the rapture or

Die in this army, but I will not get out, sell out,

Be talked out, or pushed out.

I am faithful, reliable, capable and dependable.

If my God needs me, I am ready, willing and able.

He can use me, because I am here!

I am a soldier. I am not a baby. I do not need to be

Pampered, petted, primed up, pumped up, picked up

Or pepped up. I am a soldier.

No one has to call me, remind me, write me, visit
Me, entice me or lure me.
I am a soldier. I am not a wimp.
I am in place, saluting my King, obeying His orders,
Praising His name and building His Kingdom!

No one has to send me flowers, gifts, food, cards,
Candy or give me handouts.
I do not need to be cuddled, cradled, cared for
Or catered to.
I am committed. I cannot have my feelings hurt bad
Enough to turn me around.
I cannot be discouraged enough to turn me aside.
I cannot lose enough to cause me to quit.

When Jesus called me into His army, I had nothing.
If I end up with nothing, I will still come out ahead.
My God will supply all my needs.
I am more than a conqueror; I will always triumph.
I can do all things through Christ.
Demons cannot defeat me. People cannot disillusion
me.
Weather cannot weary me-Sickness cannot stop me.

Battles cannot beat me. Money cannot buy me.
Governments cannot silence me. I am a soldier.
Even death cannot destroy me. For when my
Commander calls me from this earthly battlefield,
He will bring me back to this world with Him.

I am a soldier in the army.
I am marching, claiming victory.
I will not give up. I will not turn around.
I am a soldier, marching heaven bound.
Here I stand!

* * *

DRESSED FOR BATTLE
(Song – Jonnie Whittington)
FULLY DRESSED IN THE ARMOR OF THE LORD
READY TO DO BATTLE WITH A MIGHTY SWORD
SATAN BETTER BEWARE – LOOK OUT FOR ME
I'M FULLY DRESSED FOR BATTLE
AND CLAIMING VICTORY!

Acknowledgements

My sincere thanks to:

Tricia Jumpp, Charlotte Pickett, and Janie Tarpley who helped me with the *Women in God's Army* seminars. Much of the material in this book came from the seminars.

Lesa Henderson who assisted with the monthly *Set Free* meetings at Alton Church of God. Another inspiration for the book.

Marietta Skeens (Mary) who encouraged, discussed and offered suggestions for the manuscript and told about the bees who built their hive under her house.

Vernelyn Haggarty (Vern) who always encourages and told me about her experiences with the armadillo.

Jason Taylor who created the cover and helped with electronics.

All the Ladies of Light who prayed for me to finish this project.

My son, Mike who gave me permission to use his testimony and gave me a lot of experience in spiritual warfare.

I love you all!

Made in the USA
Columbia, SC
01 December 2024

47357510R00119